Self-Made Woman

Self-Made Woman

A STORY OF STRUGGLE, SURVIVAL AND SUCCESS

ANNE LENNOX-MARTIN,
WITH JOHNNY ACTON

StoryTerrace

This book has been written in good faith from my personal memories. I apologise if anyone remembers things differently or thinks I have been unfair.

Text Johnny Acton, on behalf of StoryTerrace

Design StoryTerrace

Copyright © Anne Lennox-Martin and StoryTerrace

Text is private and confidential

First print August 2021

StoryTerrace

www.StoryTerrace.com

CONTENTS

FOREWORD

Almost 20 years ago, when I was editing a facilities management magazine, someone suggested I interview Anne Lennox-Martin. I'd only met her the once, but she'd come across as a warm, fun person and, as one of the few well-known women in the male-dominated facilities management sector, she was an ideal person to profile in the magazine.

The interview started like any other until I asked the classic question, "How did you get into facilities management?" Anne started to tell her story. At some point, I put down my pen and stopped taking notes. My photographer, who had been busy snapping pictures of us talking, also paused and we simply sat and listened to the incredible story that you'll hear over the following pages.

It's a story of trauma, a story of hard work and hard times. A story of a woman kept in servitude who never gave up on herself or others and who fought every day to become who she is. Above all, it's a story of hope, joy and love, the life story of someone with a huge heart who has never stopped giving back. It's a celebration of survival and of finding happiness. It's a joy to read.

Thank you, Anne, for having the courage to talk about

your experiences – good and bad. I hope this story is as inspiring to others as it was to me when I first heard it almost 20 years ago.

Cathy Hayward
Chairman and Founder of Magenta Associates
Former Editor of *FM World*
July 2021

INTRODUCTION

If you like your women soft and nice
If you like them made from sugar and spice
If you like them willing
If you like them weak
Don't come round and see me
Cos I'm not who you seek

(Chorus) *No! I'm a self-made woman*
And I know my own mind
Well it ain't made me easy
And it ain't made me kind!

– Anne Lennox-Martin, *'Self-Made Woman'*

Well, let's make a start! Why write a book about your life? Much of my story has been about bloody-minded resilience and picking myself up after setbacks. Now I am in my seventies and life has been good to me for some time, I can look back and take pride in that young girl and woman who survived and lived to tell the tale.

When chatting with friends and colleagues, as you do, over and over again through the years people have said, "Wow – you should write a book." So here it is! If you are reading this now, you must be curious. Either you know me, have heard of me, or maybe you just liked the cover. Whoever you are, welcome to my world! I hope you find it interesting. The psychotherapist who literally saved my life in the late 80s told me once that I should go back and hug that girl who used to be me. Strangely, my eyes are still filling with tears as I write that. The overwhelming memory I have of the bad times is feeling so alone. So this book is a hug for myself! If you value hugs, read on...

Some people have described my life as 'Dickensian'. It's certainly been a hell of a rollercoaster. I've been 'out of the frying pan and into the fire' more times than I care to remember. My home life as a child was awful – I was abused by my grandfather and desperate to get away from the family as soon as possible – so I went off with the first man I could and ended up falling into the clutches of the Scientologists. To escape from them, I ran off with my husband's best man, who had lured me from Carlisle to London under false pretences. After getting away from him, I briefly ended up living on a park bench with two small children. Then I got a job as a live-in cleaner and thought I had landed on my feet. Instead, I wound up spending 15 years somewhere between domestic servitude and slavery.

Yet, in the midst of all this, I managed to launch a

successful career as a folk singer, and had more than my allotted 15 minutes of fame as a spokesperson for a charity for single-parent families. And eventually, I found my vocation in facilities management (FM). But no sooner had I secured my dream job than I had a catastrophic nervous breakdown, which ultimately turned out to be the making of me. And so on, and so on.

I've often wondered how I've got through everything life has thrown my way. But somewhere inside, I always had the conviction that I would get where I was meant to be. Whatever 'prison' I found myself in, and there were plenty, I told myself, "I WILL get out of this. If I have to wait, I'll wait, but I'll do it in the end. I deserve better and this is not the Anne I was destined to be. Up with this I will not put." It was a survival mechanism, but it worked. And at some level, I always felt I was special. The problem was getting the opportunity to prove it, both to myself and the rest of the world. Until I was 40, all that mattered was finding a way to escape from whatever situation I was in at the time.

Actually, I'm not telling the whole truth when I say I don't know how I survived. Something happened when I was at junior school that acted like a protective talisman, seeing me through the traumas and challenges that were to come. I'm hesitant to tell you about it because you'll probably think I'm crazy. But as you'll discover, I'm an open book (pun intended) – sometimes too open for my own good. And whether what I'm about to describe really objectively happened or just took place in my head, it's one of the most powerful and vivid experiences I've ever had.

We used to do a thing called 'Music with Movement', which involved a teacher turning on the radio, and a BBC person with a plummy 1950s accent telling us to pretend to be trees or animals and so on. We did it in the school gym, which was probably three times higher than an ordinary classroom. I remember running around in a circle with the other kids in my knickers and little top – I must have been about eight – and hearing the announcer say, "Jump like a gazelle! Jump higher. Jump higher!" So, I leapt as high as I could, and I swear to God I touched the ceiling. It's as clear as anything. The roof tiles had little holes in them, and I can remember the physical feel of them as if I'm running my hands over them now. It was a complete out-of-body experience. I looked down on the other children, still running around in a circle, and thought "I must be a god! I can do anything!" And then, suddenly, I was back down with the rest of them again.

I don't know what you'll make of that – on the face of it, I'll admit an eight-year-old girl jumping 25 feet seems unlikely – but it's my truth, and the feeling that anything is possible has stayed with me ever since. And, on the whole, my life has proved it to be correct. This is a story with a happy ending, insofar as such a thing can ever be true. It's a tale that I hope will provide hope for people who find themselves in hopeless-seeming predicaments, like I have so often in the past. I also plan, in the course of telling it, to show how – contrary to popular perception (if you've even thought about the subject at all) – facilities management can be sexy. In my own case, it's been a kind of salvation. But there's a whole lot to tell before we get to that.

1

SKELETONS

Rock-a-bye baby on the treetop
When the wind blows, the cradle will rock.

– Nursery Rhyme, Trad.

My childhood was downright weird, frankly: a combination of Victorian discipline, acute family dysfunction and isolation. My brother, sister and I used to say that no one could ever understand what it was like except us. But it's not much good taking that line in an autobiography, so I'll do my best to describe it!

Our parents were second cousins. He came from Suffolk, she from Scotland, where her father was a head gardener near Troon in Ayrshire. They got married at the beginning of the war. My mother continued to live in Scotland, where she had my sister, Phyllis, in 1943 and my brother, Alex, in

1946, but when my father was demobbed, he didn't want to live with his parents-in-law, who had both had Presbyterian upbringings and were very, very strict. So, they moved to Kent, where I was born in 1948, at Joyce Green Hospital in Dartford.

There were skeletons in the closets of both families, particularly my father's. My mother thought that something must have happened to him during the war, because apparently, he had come back a different person. My sister's theory was that it was because he'd been promoted to the rank of sergeant major. My mother said maybe he'd had an affair in Italy, which was where he was posted, or perhaps he'd suffered some other kind of trauma? Nobody knows. But there was already something very dark in his background, though I didn't find out about it until I was 17.

I was doing my family tree – a fascinating process – and went to visit an elderly relative who I'd never met before. We called her 'Aunt Rose', but she was actually my great-great-aunt, so she was very ancient indeed. Anyway, we started talking, and I said, "Can you tell me when my father's mother died, because I need to fill in the date?" And she said, "Oh, is Mabel dead then?" I almost fell off my chair. We'd all grown up to think our grandmother had died at some unspecified point when my father was a boy, whereupon my grandfather had married another woman – a snotty cow, frankly – who we knew as 'Auntie Kett'.

So then, of course, it all came out. Rose told me that Mabel had fallen in love with another man and run off with him. My grandfather had then presented my father, who would have been about 15 or 16 at the time (he was born in 1920), with an ultimatum. "You can either go with her," he said, "in which case you will never see me again, or you can stay with me, in which case you will never see her again."

Goodness knows what this must have done to my father's head. In any case, he chose to stay with my grandfather, who proceeded to destroy every single photo of my grandmother he could find in the house. "We will never speak of her again," he announced, and they didn't. My father went to his grave believing that he was an only child, though in fact Mabel had remarried following her divorce from his father, and had a son and a daughter, who were therefore his half siblings. While I was writing this chapter, my sister and I had the longest talk of our lives about our childhood. I found out that when our father died, she had been given some family photos. One of them, which I have never seen, shows our grandparents getting married. My father must have somehow managed to hide and keep it!

The net effect of all this was that my father was very close to my grandfather, and not always in the healthiest of ways. He was completely driven – that's where I must have got that from – and very ambitious. When he came back from the war, he returned to his job as a railway booking clerk, and by the time he retired he was head of PR for British

Rail Sea Ferries. So he was very much self-made. Yet he was strangely dependent on his father, who he used to go to for advice about everything. He would have wanted to buy his own house anyway, because he had 'trajectory', but my grandfather strongly encouraged him to do it and helped him out with the purchase financially. Whether he felt this gave him some sort of rights over our family I don't know. He certainly acted as though he had them, as we will see.

My mother was completely different. Like my father, she had grown up in a council house, but she was totally unambitious and didn't want to move out of our one at all. In fact, as I was horrified to discover, she wasn't even allowed to view the property that my father ended up buying. Along with the rest of us, she was just told that we were moving, three weeks before the event, and that it was a fait accompli. That's the way it worked with my parents. My father made all the decisions.

Not that I would describe my mother as meek. She was very strict, in her own way, and brought us up thoroughly 'proper'. She was adamant about things, and extremely judgemental. There were no hugs and kisses in our family, and no one ever spoke of love. But we didn't really know what we were missing as we grew up, because we'd never known things any other way. I had a flashback the other day that reminded me what life was like back then. I was having a sneezing fit at home, and after every sneeze I'd apologise frantically, saying, "Sorry, sorry!" as if I'd done something terrible. "Why do you keep saying 'sorry'?" my husband, Vin, said. About an hour later, after he'd gone to bed, I suddenly found myself back by the kitchen sink in our house in Dartford, with my mother saying exactly the same thing to me. It was so vivid. I understood then why I'd said sorry so much as a child. It was to try to prevent myself from being slapped or hit. I cried and cried when I realised that, even after all these years.

My mother never understood what I did as an adult and didn't really want to. She wouldn't come to any of my gigs for example, unlike my father, who at least managed to make it to one of them. And she was pretty dour. She'd sometimes let us play cards, which she found deliciously naughty, but there was never any alcohol allowed in the house, except at Christmas, when she'd drink a tiny glass of some ginger concoction or a snowball.

There was a softer side to her too – she loved nature, and used to take us on walks where she'd teach us the names of all the butterflies and birds and wildflowers. And we had a shared love of gardening, which I was able to write about for her funeral, when I couldn't think of much else positive to say (I had all kinds of resentments towards her, which we'll come to later). But she was scared stiff of my father. In fact, we all were. He was an amazing man in many ways, but he was a total control freak.

To give you an example, we were absolutely forbidden to flush the toilet by my parents' bedroom at night in case the noise from the water tank above woke them up. Then there was the rigmarole about watching television, when we eventually got one. We were on no account permitted to sit on our father's armchair, even if he was at work, and had to perch on uncomfortable stools. "That's father's chair, that's mother's chair, and those are where you sit." There were all kinds of rules that had to be followed when he wasn't there, so he'd know what we were doing at all times. "Just wait till your father gets home" was a common cry. We'd be scared into submission, as the hard slaps we'd get otherwise were quite painful.

Perhaps the most damaging way in which our father's need to control our lives manifested itself was that we weren't allowed to have any friends. I remember thinking it perfectly normal to have to play teddy bears with the boy next door through the fence between our houses, because I didn't know anything different. We could ride our scooters on the pavements around the flower bed outside the front of our house, or in our front garden, but that was about it until I was seven or eight.

Then my mother finally let us visit the girl who lived on the other side of the house, who was my brother's age and had a swing in her garden. I don't think she ever told my father though, as he wouldn't have liked it. We were allowed to go to the birthday parties of children from school but never to ask them back to our own. And of course, after a couple of years of non-reciprocation, the invitations started drying up. I did have a friend called Jean, who I'd hang around in the playground with and so on, but she was the only one.

You might think that the ban on outside friends would have made us siblings close to each other, but we were quite the opposite. If you asked me how I got on with them, I'd have to say, "I didn't." We were never encouraged to be a family together. When I had my breakdown, I had a wonderful psychotherapist who thought this might have had something to do with my grandfather grooming us – a 'divide and rule' sort of thing.

I shared a room with my sister, but we used to fight like cats when we were young, going at each other with our nails. As we both grew up, I remember her doing the 'big sister' bit, taking me up to London to see the ballet for example. But we were never close – she was five years older than me. And I just hated my brother, although we became very close before he died. We never had fun together as a family.

The only exceptions were Christmas, which my mother always made sure was special – she'd do lots of great baking and we'd all get involved in making paper decorations – and New Year's Eve, when we'd go round to my father's Aunt Marjorie's house. She and her husband, Uncle Mick, knew how to enjoy themselves, and God we'd have a good time playing squeak piggy squeak and pinning the tail on the donkey! I couldn't say the same of our annual summer holidays staying with my mother's parents in Troon, though.

Everything was very odd up there, although it's hard to put my finger on exactly how. But I do remember going to the local swimming pool and listening to 'Itsy Bitsy Teeny Weeny Yellow Polka Dot Bikini' blaring out of the pool radio.

So, I had a very lonely childhood. I probably had a very active imagination – I remember making up endless stories about my paper doll collection, which was quite the thing in those days – but they were all taken away from me when we moved in 1960, so my childhood was disposed of in a heartless fashion. My father didn't want any children's mess spoiling his lovely new home, thank you very much. Everything we'd had as children was given away to the local hospital or the jumble sale. I read and read though, which was something my mother was very good at encouraging, taking me to the library and so on. Later, I taught myself to play the guitar. I used to spend hours practising and singing in my room.

Music was my main outlet, in fact, although I also took to writing poetry. I always had the ability to entertain others and be a bit of a performer. As a very small girl, I remember charging people 3d. to listen to me singing from a sandpit. My mother used to call me a terrible show-off. It was a front in a way – as you will see, I've always been able to present an extrovert, competent face to the world, even when inside I've been falling apart. But music was a lifesaver for me then, as it would be at several critical periods in my life. My brother and I sang together in the local church choir, and the radio was always on in the background at home, so I learned all the popular songs of the day. As I got older, I used to have to sneak round to some cockney neighbours to get my musical fix. They used to have sing-songs around the piano, with lots of great old music hall songs.

My brother and sister suffered particularly badly from my father's way of parenting. Because I was the youngest, I was a witness to it, but it wasn't particularly aimed at me. Maybe that's why I can remember so many things. Phyllis says her memory is completely blank before the age of 14 or so, and Alex was the same way.

The rows over my brother were just awful. I truly believe that my father saw him as a threat in some way. He couldn't relate to him at all. He used to hit us all – I wouldn't call it physical abuse because in those days everyone slapped their children – but Alex definitely got the worst of it. One time, when he was about 10, he was caught shoplifting and brought home by a policeman. My sister and I were sent upstairs while my father talked to the constable. As soon as he left, all hell broke loose. We could hear our parents shouting at each other and Alex crying. There was an approved school across from where we lived, and my father said, "Right, I'm taking you across there and you're not coming back." Then he put my brother's coat on him, grabbed his ear, and dragged him out of the house by it, with my mother screaming hysterically.

This was intended to give him a fright and he did bring

him back in the end, but they kept fighting right through Alex's teenage years. I remember my father refusing to speak to him directly, and saying to my mother, "Will you ask your son to pass me the salt?" That was after some relatively minor offence. When he was caught smoking at 17, he was thrown out of the house for the day. Finally, when my father found some condoms in my brother's drawer when he was 19, he threw him out permanently. I was the last one left.

It was all very bleak. But before we move on into my troubled adolescence, there's one other 'miracle' I need to tell you about. It affected me at least as positively as the 'touching the roof of the gym' episode, because it proved to me that everything could suddenly change for the better.

It happened during year two at school, when I would have been six or seven. We'd got past the 'playing in the sand and pretending to go to the post office' phase, and the teacher had started writing sums on the blackboard, which we were supposed to write down in our exercise books and do as homework. The next day, you would swap books with your desk partner and mark each other's work as the teacher read out the answers. And I used to get every single question wrong. I was really upset about this, because I had an innate sense that I wasn't stupid and so I couldn't understand what was happening. Then one day, for some reason or other, I found myself at a desk at the front of the class, rather than further back where I usually sat.

The teacher pointed to a sum on the blackboard and

said, "Anne, tell me what this plus this is." I gave her the right answer. "Oh, OK," she said, looking slightly puzzled. "Now tell me what this plus this is." Once again, I answered correctly. Suddenly, it was as if a lightbulb lit up in her head. "From now on, you sit at the front of the class, Anne," she told me.

As you've probably worked out for yourself by now, I was actually very short-sighted, but no one had noticed this before – certainly not me, because I'd never been any other way. From where I usually sat, I hadn't been able to see the board properly, so I'd been copying all the sums down wrongly. It turned out that I usually got what I'd actually written in my exercise book right, but the child responsible for marking my homework just put crosses by my answers when the teacher said something different.

Naturally, after making this discovery, my teacher sent a note to my mother. She then took me to her opticians, who gave me a horrible pair of NHS glasses. I remember walking out of the shop with them on, squealing in wonder: "I can see the number on that bus, Mummy, I can see it!" Up until that moment, I'd been able to see enough to read a book, but not much further than that. Now everything was clear and bright. Suddenly my world had been transformed, and not for the last time.

Sister Phyllis, brother Alex and me at three months, Dartford

My maternal grandparents in Scotland

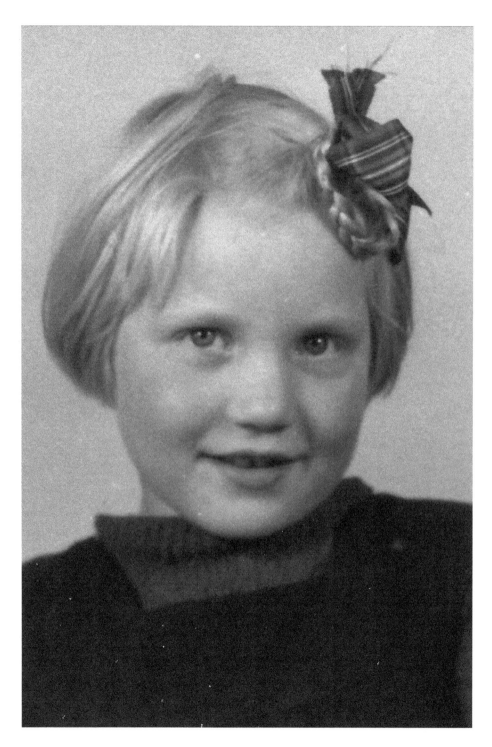

My school photo five/six years old

2

WINTER

The coldness, the harsh bitterness
Of it all.
You might say it was beautiful,
The snow I mean,
But for me it was a relentless foe
A thing despised and feared.
…
The treachery, the falsehood of it,
Hidden ice, broken bones.

I am young. Winter for me should be a joy
But I cannot,
I cannot,
The rain and the snow are too like tears,
The naked trees, too like old age
To cheer me.

wrote that poem when I was 14. It was very well received at school – my teacher wrote, "This is a most excellent poem which carries its strong, sustained imagery to a final successful conclusion... What a cry of despair!" The last comment was certainly correct. As you have no doubt worked out from the contents of 'Winter', my life wasn't a barrel of laughs when I wrote it. In fact, it was one of my more cheerful poems! This wasn't just standard adolescent angst either, although goodness knows that can be bad enough. No, by this stage what I describe as 'the blackness' had descended.

I may have told my second husband about my grandfather abusing me, and my daughters as they became teenagers as part of a general warning about men. I also tried to tell my mother when I was 17, whereupon she slapped me in the face (I've never really been able to forgive her). Apart from that, I never mentioned it to anyone until my breakdown almost three decades later. But since then, I've spoken about it quite openly, because I think it's important for people who have been through that kind of nightmare to come forward and not bottle it up inside. In fact, I was on the BBC's *Listening Project* with a friend, sharing our experiences of being abused as children.

If I was being unjustifiably charitable, I might say, "At least he waited until I'd hit puberty," but I was so young when that happened that it's neither here nor there really. I had my first period when I was nine. Fortunately, I had some vague idea what was going on, because there was a girl at school who'd started even earlier than me. I just remember waking up to find blood on my sheets and telling my mother.

"Lie back," she told me, and then she started poking around in there. "Yes, I thought so," she said. "It's all part of being a woman. Get yourself dressed and I'll go and find you something." When she came back, she put a huge, very uncomfortable sanitary belt on me, shoved a pad between my legs and off I went to school. That evening, she handed me a pamphlet and left me to read it. That was about it as far as my home 'sex education' went. The booklet put me in the picture to some extent, but its diagrams of the male and female organs were not attached to bodies. Consequently, I formed the idea that men kept these things in their pockets and got them out when they wanted to get girls pregnant. I wish I'd been able to hold onto this naive belief for longer.

By the time I was 11, I had a 36C bust, but of course my mother wouldn't let me wear a bra. By this stage we had moved, and I had one term in the village school before going on to the Tonbridge Girls Grammar School. So, there I was running around innocently with these things jiggling about all over the place, and the teachers treating me like a little tart. "How dare you play with the boys!" they'd tut-tut at me. At my old school, we had all grown up together, so nothing had ever been noticed or said. This was very different.

Meanwhile, the village children teased me mercilessly. In the end, my mother relented, but only because she had to.

It was around this time that my grandfather made his move. Up until then I'd adored him. He'd grown up in Laxfield in Suffolk, where there is a whole graveyard full of Selsbys, which was my maiden name. We used to visit my grandfather ('Poppa') and Auntie Kett every second week, and the following fortnight they would come to ours, so he had plenty of opportunity to initiate the abuse. The first time it happened, he put his hand over my mouth. There was no need for him to say "don't you dare tell anyone about this" – I understood that immediately.

The first year or so of the abuse is a bit of a blur to me, simply because of the horror of it. But I know that my grandfather quickly developed a routine. I was the youngest, so I'd go to bed hours before my sister and brother. At a suitable moment, he'd leave the living room, where everyone was watching TV, and pretend he was going to the toilet. He'd open and close the door of it very loudly, then he'd tiptoe into my room and abuse me. He never actually penetrated me, but that was about the only thing he didn't do. When I was writing this book, one of the questions I pondered was "When did you have your first kiss?" I couldn't for the life of me remember. Then I worked out why. The answer was that it had been 'given' to me by my grandfather. I remember his tongue feeling like a slimy lizard. No wonder I'd blocked out the memory.

The awfulness of the situation was magnified by the fact that there was absolutely no one for me to talk to about it. Not that people spoke about that sort of thing in those days – there was no Childline or anything – and of course it's still incredibly difficult for the victims to ask for help today. Leigh (pronounced 'Lie'), the posh village we'd moved to because my father was going up in the world, was a long way from the council estate where we'd lived previously, so I was completely cut off from everyone I'd known there. And I didn't have the kind of relationship with my sister where we shared our troubles, though many years later she revealed that she'd always been wary of both my grandfather and father.

The abuse went on for three years. By the time I was 14, my grandfather had started picking me up from school, taking me into the woods and making me give him blowjobs. It was horrible. Then one day, my parents told me that my mother was going into hospital for an operation on her varicose veins. My brother would be staying with my father, and my sister was working by now, so she could take care of herself, but I was going to have to stay with my grandparents.

"I'm not going," I told them flatly.

"Why not?" they said. "Of course you are." Not surprisingly, I felt completely unable to tell them the real reason. I had no other choice, so I went.

The very first night, it was the same old routine. He went to bed with his wife, then after about half an hour, he got up, opened the bathroom door, closed it again, and came into my room. I was wide awake, because I knew what was coming. Only this time, I sat bolt upright on the bed and said, "If you come near me, I'm going to scream!" And I remember him looking at me, shaking his head, and saying, "But I thought you liked it." Then he walked out, went back to bed and never touched me again.

You might think this would have been a moment of triumph and relief for me, but in fact I was left feeling absolutely dreadful. "I could have done that at any time," I thought to myself. "Why didn't I do it sooner?" That self-accusation went round and round in my head for years. I suppose it was a classic example of 'victim's guilt'. I still feel physically sick when I consider that I could have saved myself all that torment if I'd just threatened to scream the first time he had tried to touch me.

There's another layer to this too. This is very difficult to write about, but I feel I must, because it's an important part of my story. And I can't speak for anyone else, but I suspect that for some victims at least, what I'm about to describe plays a significant role in how sexual abuse messes with their heads. The fact is, my grandfather hadn't been a hundred percent wrong when he'd said, "But I thought you liked it." Amid all the outrage and sense of betrayal, on a purely physical level a part of me HAD enjoyed it. In many ways, that was the worst side effect of all. I had been prematurely sexually awakened, and once that genie is out of its bottle, it isn't easy to put it back. The guilt about that was phenomenal.

One of the ways I attempted to deal with it was by becoming an outrageous flirt. I remember squirming on the lap of my mother's brother, who was in his thirties and very good looking. Frankly, I was trying to bring myself off. "You really shouldn't be doing that," he said, virtually pushing me off him, but even that didn't set off alarm bells in the family. Denial and looking the other way run deep, I guess. Then there was the delivery man at the village shop where I took a Saturday job when I was 14. He was in his fifties or sixties, and almost a caricature of a dirty old man, and I'm ashamed to say I let him finger me in the storeroom. That took my sense of self-disgust to a whole new level.

I was very confused and overwhelmed with feelings that I had no idea how to cope with. One day, on the way to school, I walked past a church and noticed that the door was open. "I'm just going to go in there and sit there for a bit," I thought to myself. Then I walked in, sat in a pew and cried my eyes out. After a while, the vicar came out and talked to me. I didn't mention the abuse, but he could see how unhappy I was. He was very kind. "We have a Bible study class which you could come to after school," he told me. "Perhaps that would help." So I took him up on the offer. In fact, I eventually got confirmed in that church.

Basically, what I was doing was trying to use religion to quell my sexual feelings. Sublimation, I think they call it. It worked for a few years. I managed to stop with the delivery man, and by the time I was 16 or 17, I had a boyfriend my own age. I wouldn't let him anywhere near me though.

The abuse wasn't the only problem within my family. By this time, my father was going up in the world, and he started nagging my mother to go to dinner parties with his bosses and so on. He wanted her to play the dutiful early-60s corporate wife, but she was very resistant, because she lacked social confidence and felt she didn't have any conversation. I remember him telling her he was ashamed of her, and from that point, he started to look down on her. My sister always stuck up for her, but much of this passed me by as I was so self-absorbed because of the abuse.

What didn't pass me by was the way my father reacted to me coming out of my room one day wearing lipstick. He wiped it off savagely with a dry flannel, bloodying my face in the process. As we have already seen, in his family, the men controlled the women, and he wasn't having his daughter going out looking like that. My reaction was to pack a bag and run away to my friend Wendy's house.

She lived in Hildenborough, which was two or three miles away, and her parents were just lovely to me. As usual, I didn't mention the abuse, but I spilled my heart out about everything else. Once I'd calmed down, her father drove me back home and told me to stay in the garden while he had a word with my parents. I don't know what he said to them, but my father never laid a finger on me after that.

I think my mother must have been impressed by his speech too, because many years later she married him! I was working as a live-in cleaner in London when my father left her, and she was in a terrible state. Then I met up with Wendy, who told me that her mother had died. "Wouldn't it be lovely if we could get the two of them together?" we said. The next thing we knew, they'd done it all by themselves! It was fantastic. They adored each other and spent seven or eight years together before he died. My mother was happier than I'd ever seen her during this period and mellowed considerably.

All that was unimaginably far in the future back then, though. In the meantime, I was still struggling to cope with the abuse and the poisonous atmosphere at home. One of the ways in which I acted it out was by starting to behave badly at school. The most disturbed thing I did was tell the school that my mother had died and that I needed to take a day off for the funeral. I kept up the pretence for a week and it was never questioned. Obviously, it was a cry for help of sorts, but Wendy told me later that she had really believed it. Then she came to my house one day, and of course my mother was there alive and well, so she decided I had gone completely mad.

Despite all these shenanigans, I was so bright that I passed all my exams. Well, maybe not all of them - I think I failed art A level, but I had never wanted to do it in the first place. My choice had been Latin, but the school had said it wouldn't fit in with the curriculum. I got distinctions in the other two though, which were English and history. And my history teacher, Mrs Thorne, was an absolute saviour.

She had this way of winkling things out of me. One day, when she announced that she wanted to take our class on a field trip, I told her my family would never let me go.

"Don't they want you to do well and go to university?" she said.

"I don't want to go there myself," I told her.

"Why ever not?" she said. "You're really bright and you'd do very well."

She wouldn't let it go and sat me down to talk it through. I explained to her that I had to get away from home, and if I went to university I'd have to carry on living there in the holidays. I didn't mention the abuse, but I told her everything else, chiefly how I didn't get on with my parents and that their attitudes were Victorian.

"Have you ever been away from home and stayed in a hotel?" she asked me. No, I told her, we never went anywhere (I didn't count the annual misery-fest in Troon). "Well I'm going away for the weekend to some friends in Devon," she said, "and I'd really like you to come with me. We're going to visit some historical places, so it'll all be part of your A level. I'm going to write to your parents and ask for their permission."

Predictably enough, my father's response to her letter was to say no. Less predictably, my mother took a different line for once in her life. "You should let her go," she said, and on this occasion she prevailed.

Mrs Thorne had a little Mini, and we meandered down to Devon in it, visiting Petworth House en route and spending a night in a hotel in Salisbury. This was the most glamorous thing that had ever happened to me, easily trumping the time my sister had given me curried beans – the last word in sophistication – when I had visited her in Tunbridge Wells after she'd started working as a librarian. But staying in a hotel was in a different league entirely, and I was in heaven.

The great thing about Mrs Thorne was that she was fascinating to talk to, and I'd never had anyone talk to me about interesting things before. At the end of the trip, I said to her, "How can I ever thank you?" Her reply was something I've never forgotten.

"Life is like a bank, Anne", she said. "When you have it, you put it in, and when you need it you take it out." I knew she wasn't talking about money, but giving and accepting help and support. "And it doesn't have to be the same person," she added. It's a lesson I've tried to apply ever since.

My grandfather in the Great War

About 11 years old at my grandparents', in the middle of the abuse

Mrs Thorne with her A level History students. I am taking the picture

3

OUT OF THE FRYING PAN
AND INTO THE FIRE

Nobody knows the trouble I've seen
Nobody knows but Jesus
Nobody knows the trouble I've seen
Glory, Hallelujah.

– Spiritual, Trad

Eventually I did get away from my parents, although there was an interim period when I was working but still living at home. And like many things in my life, my professional career started with me being plunged straight in the deep end.

I had wanted to train as a nurse at one stage, and had told the careers officer at school that I intended to become a professional singer (an idea that was pooh-poohed as beyond ridiculous). In fact, what happened was I became a civil servant in the Department of Health and Social Security. I started with a probationary period as an executive officer in Tunbridge Wells. I was 18 at the time – 18! – and put in charge of a team of four women and one man, all in their forties or fifties.

You can imagine how they felt about their new teenager boss. They were absolutely horrible to me, and used to take pleasure in guiding me the wrong way and getting me into all sorts of trouble. I understood their attitude though, and didn't hold it against them. I just carried on trying to do the best work I could.

One thing in particular did wonders for my confidence. (You may be starting to detect a pattern here. So often in my story, I'm facing what seem to be insurmountable challenges, then something comes along that reminds me that I have it in me to overcome them and get where I'm meant to be.) My team used to take it in turns to be on the customer service desk.

One day, when the man in my team was on duty there, he came into the office where I was sitting with the women and said, "There's this guy downstairs I can't do anything with. You're going to have to come and sort it out."

"What's the story?" I said.

"Well, it's this big black fellow, he's got a sore thumb, and he's trying to claim sickness benefit," he told me. "And I'm not having it. So he's threatened me and asked to see my manager. Be careful," he added as I made my way out of the door, "because he's very big." All the women were giggling like schoolgirls. "This is going to be fun," they must have been thinking.

Now I don't know how or why I was able to deal with this situation, but somehow I was. I went downstairs, and there was this huge guy looking distinctly unhappy. "Mr so-and-so, I understand there's some difficulty," I said to him. He started shouting and swearing at me, getting so worked up that I was relieved that all the furniture was screwed down (angry claimants used to sometimes come in and thump the staff, and the DHSS wanted to make sure that's all they could do).

"Look," I told him, "I can see you're really upset. Why don't we go and have a chat about it somewhere quieter?" Then I led him to the interview room, where there was a panic button in case of emergency.

When we got there, I didn't do what I was supposed to, which was to make damned sure that I sat nearest the door with him safely the other side of the desk. Instead, some instinct told me to position us the other way around, so I was on the inside 'hosting' him. "I want you to tell me everything that's been going on with you," I began and almost immediately he started to calm down. Then it all came out. It turned out that he was a chef. He'd cut himself whilst working, then the wound had got infected, and his employers quite rightly wouldn't allow him back in the kitchen until it healed. He was trying to claim sickness benefit, perfectly reasonably. He'd been off work for two weeks, with no benefit coming in and a young family to support.

"What I'm going to do," I told him, "is arrange for you to get a cash payment now to tide you over, then you'll get a giro in a couple of days to cover the rest of it. Is that OK?" When I looked across at him, he was staring at me with tears running down his face. All he could say was, "Oh ma'am.... Oh ma'am!" Because someone had finally listened to him.

When I walked back into the office, they were all sitting there with their mouths wide open, because they'd assumed I would fail miserably. I was extremely hot on racism, and I took the chap in my team to one side and said, "Look, you really ought to check before you make assumptions about people." I remember feeling very proud of myself that day.

After my probationary period in Tunbridge Wells was over, I got a job at the DHSS in Balham. At first, I stayed in a freezing cold B&B, owned by a couple of old spinsters, which I absolutely hated. Then a friend suggested that we get a bedsit together, so I ended up living with her in Croydon. In fact, and I'm terribly conflicted about revealing this, we had a bit of a lesbian relationship for a while. Even now, I find myself feeling very ashamed of this. I don't know why, because I'm the furthest thing from homophobic and have lots of lesbian and gay friends. But I'm not sure I've even told my husband, Vin, about it before. Still, what's the point of an autobiography if you don't tell it like it was? I think it happened because I was so highly sexed but also desperately trying to stay away from men.

I didn't manage to avoid them for long though. This girl, Deb, was a technical assistant at a chemicals company, and she introduced me to a colleague called Ian, who was a chemical engineer 11 years older than me. He was very attentive from the word go, and I was flattered, because I couldn't believe that any man would want me. I must have been quite taken with him too, but I think I'd have been taken with anyone who I thought could provide me with a way out. I'd left home physically but I was still tied to the past psychologically. And despite everything that had happened, I still felt I needed the protection of a man. It was a very ambivalent time for me. On the one hand, it was the 60s, the era of demonstrations, flower power and the pill, and I was performing all the protest songs and so on at my semi-professional gigs. On the other hand, I'd had this strict Victorian upbringing, so I didn't really know if I was coming or going.

I'm not sure Ian did either. He'd had a pretty strange upbringing himself. He came from Cumbria, where his mother was a 'white' witch and his father a 'black' one, and since his teens he'd been involved in something I'd never heard of called Scientology. But none of that mattered to me. All I cared about was that he offered me a potential escape route.

As I say, I knew nothing about the religion, if you can call it that (and there have been numerous legal arguments about whether you can or can't). There were no celebrity Scientologists like Tom Cruise or John Travolta back then, and although the organisation was about to become very notorious and controversial, when I first got involved it was still operating largely under the radar. Scientology had grown out of a belief system called Dianetics, which was developed in the late 1940s and early 50s by an American science fiction writer called L Ron Hubbard.

You have to go through a process called 'auditing', which allegedly gradually clears away all the traumas in your past. This is done with the aid of a device called an E-meter, which is a bogus lie detector machine. You have to hold what look like a couple of tin cans, while a senior Scientologist interrogates you about your life and thoughts until you give the 'right' answers. There are endless 'levels' you have to rise through, and on each occasion you have to pay for the privilege, but eventually, you become what in Scientologist parlance is described as 'Clear'. This means that you have supposedly been cleansed of all unwanted emotions and influences from the past. You are now what is called an 'Operating Thetan', although there are several levels of that too. By that stage, you allegedly have godlike control over matter, space and time. I never believed a word of it, even when I got deeply drawn into the movement, but I played along because I didn't feel I had any choice. As you will see, the Scientologists were very coercive, and that's putting it mildly.

At the time I met Ian, he was living in a one-bedroom flat with three other Scientologists in Oxted, West Sussex. There was an Operating Thetan called Alan, who was quite high up in the organisation, a lovely guy called John, and a woman named Mary who I remember as being very difficult. One day, I went to visit them there, and lost my virginity to Ian (despite the abuse and the delivery man, I had never gone the full way before) in a room filled with his housemates. It was just horrible, but that was how they lived – you weren't supposed to have a private life. And once that had happened, that was it, I was one of them. In those days, you followed the man, it was that simple.

As soon as I'd slept with Ian, I knew I was going to have to marry him. For reasons you will understand by now, I was already thoroughly messed up in the head about sex, so I felt incredibly guilty. But there was another layer to it too. A few years before, my sister had got pregnant, and this had caused dreadful rows with my father, even though she and her boyfriend wanted to get married. It had been horrendous, and my mother had said, "Don't you ever dare get pregnant yourself, because it will kill your father, and I'll hold you responsible." So, of course, the minute I lost my virginity I was scared stiff, because I thought I could be pregnant. I loved my father, and genuinely felt that if I didn't get married the world would end.

To complicate matters, the Scientologist position is that your parents aren't important. Unless they're members of the cult, or supportive like Ian's mother (to whom it probably seemed a lot less wacky given her witch stuff), you're supposed to cut off all contact with them. In fact, they make you write them horrible 'goodbye' letters and swear to never see them again. But despite all that, within a couple of weeks I'd taken Ian down to meet my parents.

I actually think they tried to be as understanding as possible, but Ian was a lot older than me and not particularly prepossessing – he wasn't at all good looking, for example – and they couldn't wrap their heads around what we were proposing at all. Obviously, I couldn't say to them, "I have to marry him because I've had sex with him." They were perfectly polite to him, but they told me, "No way, you are not marrying him. You need to wait a couple of years before you even think about it."

The pressure from the Scientologists to send my parents their 'farewell' letter combined with my dread of becoming pregnant made me absolutely determined to get married to Ian. But I was only 19, and the law in England at the time was that you couldn't get married under the age of 21 without parental consent. Ian's flatmate, Alan, who came from Scotland, pointed out that the law there was different. Provided you were over 16 and had been in the country for at least three weeks, you didn't need parental consent.

So the farewell letter was sent with no forwarding

address, and then we took the train to Scotland. Much later, I learned that my sister and her husband had spent many hours driving around Croydon looking for me, or at least trying to find out what had happened to me. I had no idea at the time how hurtful this must have been for my parents. It was a dreadful thing to do to them and they didn't deserve it. But that was how the Scientologists corrupted people. After receiving my letter, my father wouldn't speak to me for years, even after I'd detached myself from the Church. It was only after he had left my mother and hatched a scheme for me to move in with her to ease his conscience that he got back in touch with me.

Alan's mother had offered to put us up in her flat in Glasgow for the required period – she thought it was all terribly romantic – so for three weeks we shared a tiny single bed. I remember sitting on it the night before the wedding thinking, "I don't want to do this… I really don't want to do this," though in the end I went through with it, of course. The whole thing felt seedy and dirty, and I couldn't get rid of this deep sense of shame. I felt ashamed all the time back then, particularly in connection with anything to do with sex. And the only reason I was getting married to Ian was that I'd had sex with him. I'm not sure I was really in love with him. I saw him as my escape clause. We'd both quit our jobs and run away together. He'd been earning £1,500 a month, which was a fortune in those days. Now I had no idea how we were going to survive.

The best man at the wedding was a friend of Ian's called Nick Goller, who will come back into the story later. I became very close to his American wife, Fran, who was a Scientologist too, but a very sensible person, unlike most of the men. After the wedding, which was in March 1968, we went back to Oxted to resume living in the flat with the others. It wasn't the ideal start to married life.

Things were very scrambled in my head by this time, as I had been indoctrinated up to 'Level Four' by Alan and Ian, with the help of some of their friends. As you go through the levels, they ask you questions while you're holding the cans, and when you answer them, if the E-meter shows a reaction they tell you that you're lying. You aren't, but they insist that the machine is never wrong. So the cans must be registering something from a past life. You've got to be open and remember it before you can progress, so you end up making up anything to get yourself to the next level. And before long, you no longer know what's true and what isn't.

We were living only a few miles down the road from Saint Hill Manor, the Church's UK headquarters, so when we returned from Scotland we were there a lot. We had no money apart from what Ian had left from when he was working. I used my last sixpence to ring and find out about benefits. Neither of us could receive unemployment benefit as we had voluntarily left work, but we did get a few emergency payments. To make them last, I would cook rice, fried onions and peas with tomato ketchup, which would keep us going for several days.

Ian was spending all his time and energy with Alan on secret matters, and the upshot was that I felt I had to go along with everything the Scientologists said. Before long, they had me handing out leaflets outside their centre in the Tottenham Court Road. They also continued auditing me on the E-meters. Unlike most people, I don't think I ever had to pay for it, because of my associations with Alan and Ian. This was just as well, as I had absolutely no money. But the process still did plenty of psychological damage.

After a few months, Alan must have fallen out badly with the powers that be at Saint Hill, because one day the Scientologists' internal police descended on the flat, herded us all into a van and drove us to the manor. When we got there, we were separated from Alan and they let John go. I don't know what happened to Mary, but I never saw her again. Ian and I were isolated in a room and placed in what was called 'liability', which meant you were deemed to be in a state of non-existence. It was like an exaggerated form of being sent to Coventry. Nobody was allowed to talk to you and you were made to wear a grey rag around your arm. It had happened to me a few times in Oxted, when the others had turned on me for reasons I've now forgotten. One time, they had confined me to the bathroom, forcing me to sleep in the bath, and carried on using the loo as though I wasn't there, which was horrendous.

While we were imprisoned in Saint Hill Manor, I was subjected to something called the Johannesburg Security Test, which was one of the toughest weapons in the Scientologists' arsenal. They told me I had to take the test to prove that I was on their side.

They began by asking a few weird but innocuous-seeming things like, "Are you on the Moon?" and "Am I an ostrich?", supposedly to test that the E-meter was working properly. Then they got down to business, bombarding me with almost a hundred questions, such as,

"Have you ever been a drug addict?"

"Have you ever been a spy for the police?"

"Do you know of any secret plans against Scientology?"

They kept on and on at me, saying, "You're lying" at almost every turn. The only way to get through it was to give them the answers they wanted. It was a horrific ordeal. But I must have passed the test, because they didn't kick me out of the Church or try to separate me and Ian.

After about a week of imprisonment and manual labour at Saint Hill Manor, we were released. Before we went back to Oxted, we spent our first night of relative freedom with a Hungarian couple who had a gorgeous baby daughter called Elana. I remember thinking, "What a lovely name." I'm not sure why she made such an impression on me – I may have been pregnant already or perhaps I was just broody (the sequence of events is a bit muddled at this stage, which is what brainwashing can do to you). But I was certainly 'in the family way' by the autumn, because it was then that I announced to Ian, "We're going to have a baby and we need to get away from these people and have an independent life."

'Folk 3', my first folk group. We appeared at the first Sevenoaks Folk Festival in 1965

Seventeen years old, soon to leave school

My first wedding to Ian with best man Nick Goller. Glasgow, March 1968

4

OPPORTUNITY KNOCKS?

My mother she trained me in the cooking and the sewing
The cleaning and the caring to make me a good wife
She taught me all the skills that my grandmother gave her
But she never taught me how to expect any other life.

— Chris Coe, *'The Rising of the Women'*

We looked around for somewhere to live in London and eventually found two rooms in Riversdale Road in Highbury, which we rented for £4 a week. The landlord and landlady lived on the ground floor and we were at the top. I was terribly ill with morning sickness in the early part of my pregnancy. I vomited about 13 times a day and became very thin, so I was all 'bump'. There was no question of me getting a job while I was in that condition, and Ian had quit work some time before, so we soon became desperately poor again. Fortunately, my symptoms improved somewhat after about three months and I was able to get a clerical job with Shell in their building in Waterloo. I got free lunches in the staff restaurant, and I was earning money, which felt wonderful and meant we could stay on in the flat, at least for the time being.

London in the 60s was just fabulous. I wrote a poem about the smell of the pavements in the sun which captures some of how I felt about living there at the time. After what had come before, it was paradise. We'd go to Kew Gardens and museums and so on. I was also able to meet up with friends occasionally, like Nigel, who had almost become my boyfriend during my last year at school. We had a shared love of music - he bought me *Sgt. Pepper* and *Hey Jude*, which of course were 'must haves' in that era. I even started seeing my mother from time to time. She had quite quickly forgiven me for cutting off contact and disappearing, and used to come up to town to visit me. She had to keep it secret from my father though.

So things were looking up, but not for long. Our landlord and lady noticed that I wasn't keeping our flat very clean or tidy, and then they found out I was pregnant. They didn't want a child living upstairs, so they asked us to leave. Back then, when you were evicted, you were evicted. There was no legal recourse whatsoever. I had no idea what was going to happen to us and was terrified.

We did have one option though. Ian had always claimed to own a house in Carlisle, and he said, "Right, I think we'll have to move up there and live in it." So off we went to Cumbria. At first, we stayed with Ian's mother and stepfather, in the grace and favour house they lived in on the estate where he was one of the farming staff. He was gorgeous – a lovely, big, gentle, country guy. His wife, Irene, by contrast, was a real live wire. She'd been a Flapper back in the 1920s and the first woman in Cumbria to own a car. She was very interesting, but a complete bag of frogs. As I mentioned earlier, she was a white witch who used her 'powers' to help people, while Ian's birth father was a black one, meaning he was more interested in the malevolent side of the dark arts. Apparently, this difference in approach was the reason they had split up.

As you can imagine, coming from a background that on the surface at least had been very conventional, the witchcraft business seemed like a complete load of bullshit to me. On the other hand, after all the Scientology stuff, I was used to being surrounded by people with wacky beliefs. So I just went along with everything!

The only islands of sanity in this circus were Ian's uncle Tom (Irene's brother) and his wife, Mary. They were just 'normal' people, as I understood normality, and terribly kind. They owned the corner chemist shop just up the road from the house we subsequently moved into.

We had virtually no money coming in – just the bare

minimum of benefits, which were a lot less generous in those days (not that they are great now). Eventually, Ian went to his father, whose 'day job' was being a local estate agent, and started doing some work for him, but things were always very tight. Yet, despite some dark moments, on the whole it was a happy phase in my life. I loved decorating the house and turning it into a proper home for us.

Then, of course, Elayna was born (I remembered the name of that Hungarian couple's lovely baby and added a 'Y' so I wasn't just copying it). I'd been looking forward to her arrival ever since I'd known I was pregnant. It meant I would finally have something of my own to love, which just felt right after everything I'd been through. I'd also done a fair bit of babysitting, so I knew what to expect. I felt quite confident about it.

I remember this wonderful signage at the hospital, which said, "Please leave your modesty here and collect it when you go." I absolutely loved that! The birth itself was amazing. I mean, it was painful, as these things tend to be, but just as Elayna came into the world, a shaft of sunlight passed through the window and across the bed. It was the most amazing thing. She was born with great big violet eyes, which she could focus immediately. The whole medical team came in to see her doing it. It was just a magical time for me.

After Elayna was born, I went back to singing pretty quickly, performing in working men's clubs as 'Anne Lennox-

Martin and her guitar'. I'd sing covers of 60s folk songs by the likes of Dylan, Joan Baez and Kris Kristofferson. Ian stayed at home to babysit, and a young man called William who worked in Ian's father's office and had a car became my roadie. Earning some cash in hand was a great treat.

One of the places William used to drive me to over the border in Lanarkshire offered me a residency. I'd play there every Saturday night. I'd be the only woman in the entire place, as women in Scotland weren't welcomed in pubs in those days. It was wall-to-wall male Rangers and Celtic fans, and while I was singing, they'd be chatting away to each other and whirring football rattles. As soon as I stopped, they would all turn around and stare at me. It was quite eerie.

You might think I would have been intimidated, but I absolutely loved it. I wasn't bad-looking in those days, and they'd keep buying me drinks because they thought it would be fun to get this young girl pissed. Eventually, I had a word with the landlord, because I couldn't afford to get drunk as I'd be playing for two hours non-stop.

"Here's what we'll do," he told me. "I'm going to put a small table behind the stage curtain. Whenever someone offers you a drink, accept it, and make sure everyone sees you take a sip. Then make a big show of putting the glass on the table, which no one will be able to see. When you get the chance, nip behind the curtain and act like you're taking a big swig. There'll be a bucket hidden back there and you just need to pour your drink into it and get ready for someone to buy you the next one!"

So that's what I did. I'd make a big drama out of it, emerging from behind the curtain licking my lips and hamming up being tipsy. The men thought I was fantastic! I became notorious for being able to hold my booze, and the drinks just kept on coming. It was a complete win-win. The landlord paid me a commission based on how many rounds I was able to persuade them to buy me, and the alcoholic guy behind the bar was happy too because at the end of the night he got to drink the contents of the bucket. It was great fun and I'd go home absolutely buzzing.

The reception I was getting at the working men's clubs was very confidence-boosting, so I applied to go on *Opportunity Knocks*, which was the *X Factor* of its day. There was an audition somewhere in the North West and I went along with William and had a great time. I found the experience fascinating. We were all gathered together in a room, then called through one by one to do our thing in front of Hughie Green, the show's presenter, who was very smarmy and spoke in a fake American accent, and the legendary producer Royston Mayoh, who went on to do everything from *This Is Your Life* to *The Kenny Everett Show*. I sang them a scout song I'd learned from Fran, the wife of our best man, Nick (she also taught me the version of 'St. James Infirmary Blues' that I still sing today). It had the catchy title *Eddie Cucha Catcha Cama, Tosta Nana Tosta Noka,*

Samma Camma Wacky Brown, which took a bit of memorising, but they seemed to really like what I did. I got a letter shortly afterwards saying that I had been accepted to appear on the show. They said that they would call on me in due course and it might be at short notice. I was featured in the local paper!

By the time I got their telegram, I was pregnant with Mickie. I remember going to the nearest phone box and telling them that I was five months pregnant, just so they would know. "Are you showing yet?" asked the woman on the other end of the phone. I told her that I was, then she said, "Hang on" and went off to speak to someone. When she came back on the line she said, "Sorry, I'm afraid we can't do it. We may hold you over until after the baby has been born, but we can't have a visibly pregnant woman on the show." I mean, can you imagine? I'm sure feminists would have plenty to say about that today! But there was no point arguing with them, and of course they subsequently lost touch with me. Missing out on *Opportunity Knocks* was a pity, but I guess it just wasn't meant to be.

Mickie was born on 27th December 1970. She came out in a great rush, so I had to have a large number of stitches. I was in hospital for 48 hours, which they insisted on in those days. When I brought her home, the Christmas tree was still up in our front room. It was the one part of the house we could keep warm, because there was a beautiful Victorian fireplace, so I slept there in a single bed with Mickie beside me in a cot, and we kept the fire going all night. I had done up the room while I was pregnant, and it was stunning, if I say so myself. I remember breastfeeding Mickie by the light of the Christmas tree and the fire, and it all being just utterly enchanting.

About three months after Mickie was born, I developed an abscess in a tooth. I was scared stiff of dentists, but the pain was so bad that I made an emergency appointment with the local dental surgery and left the girls with our new next-door neighbours, Joe and Annie, who would become Mickie's godparents. I was in such a state that the dentist gave me an injection to calm me down before he removed the tooth with no anaesthetic. When I asked him how long it was going to be before I was allowed to walk home, because I had to get back to breastfeed my baby, they said, "Oh no, you can't breastfeed after that injection."

At this point, I went completely insane. "You can't do this to me!" I shouted at them. "She's never had anything else but breast milk! She'll starve!" I rushed home in a total panic, then I grabbed Elayna and Mickie and put them in the pram. Then, still feeling very groggy from the injection, I wheeled it to the local phone box at top speed and called my mother. It was instinctive.

"Please come and help me," I begged her. "I don't know what to do!"

And she just said, with ice in her voice, "Well, you've made your bed, now you've got to lie in it." Then she put down the phone. It was utterly devastating. I'd never felt more rejected and alone. What I didn't know then, but was later told by my sister, was that this was around the time my father was leaving her, so she was bitter and in her own world. But that was no help to me in that moment.

As I was making my way back down the road in a state of total despair, I saw a light on in the pharmacy stores behind Ian's aunt and uncle's corner shop. I realised they must be doing some stock taking, so I hammered on the door. When Mary came to answer it, she saw the tears running down my face. "What's the matter?" she said. "What's happened? Come on in and tell me everything."

It was lovely and cosy in there. She sat me down and I told her about the injection and how I couldn't breastfeed Mickie and was terrified about what might happen to her. Then both girls started to cry – it was just awful. At this point, her husband Tom made a discreet exit. Mary was wonderfully matter-of-fact. She gave me all the baby bottle equipment I would need and showed me how it was all done. I felt she was the mother I had always wished for.

When I'd calmed down a bit, I started talking to her about the house, and how I wanted to get it properly sorted to make a home for the family. Then she dropped the bombshell.

"You know it's not Ian's house, don't you?" she asked me.

"Yes it is," I insisted. "He told me it was."

"I'm afraid it isn't," she said. "It's his mother's house.

Irene lets you stay there for free, but strictly speaking you should be paying her rent."

So Ian had been lying to me all along. No wonder he'd been so resistant when I'd suggested selling the house so we could buy somewhere, run it as a B&B and earn some money. I was absolutely horrified. If you couldn't trust the person to whom you were married to tell you the truth, who could you trust?

It was that night that I decided once and for all that I was going to have to leave Ian. I had been getting increasingly desperate, because he had started getting involved with Scientology again. I'd made him stop when we'd moved to London.

"I don't want anything more to do with it", I'd told him. "We are NOT going to have children brought up as Scientologists," When we'd moved to Carlisle, he'd been OK for a while, but then he got back in touch with John, the guy from the flat in Oxted, who came up to visit us. Soon they were opening up a Cumbria branch together. I got very upset and angry.

"I don't want you to do this," I told Ian. But he took no notice. It was like dealing with a relapsing addict. The final straw came when he said he wanted to put Elayna on the E-meters. She was two at the time and I put my foot down. "I'm not having it," I told him.

Once again, I felt a terrible trap closing in on me. The blackness was returning. It had first descended on me when my grandfather had started abusing me, and although it had sometimes receded into the background, the threat of it had never gone away completely. Now it was back with a vengeance.

It's not an easy feeling to describe. The best I can do is to say that it's like the bottom falling out of my world and a driving force for survival taking over. There's an absolute certainly that I have to move on or perish, but at the same time, I've no idea how to do it. There's a terrible fear that this time I might not be able to get out of the situation I'm in, yet it's crystal clear to me that I must. I'm not even sure that I'm going to be able to survive the feeling. I just know, to repeat a phrase I used earlier, that 'up with this I will not put'.

So I started to plot my escape. I'd begun talking to the only people I felt I could trust, who were Nick Goller, our best man, and his wife, Fran, who had always been kind to me. They were Scientologists, but I didn't know anyone else or feel I could be open about my intentions with our neighbours or Ian's relatives. Nick must have come up to Carlisle to talk to Ian about this new Scientology chapter. I took him aside and confided in him, telling him that the marriage was over and that I had to leave. He told me he had an aunt in Richmond who could do with some live-in help.

"If you want me to, I can ask her if she'd be willing to offer you a job," he suggested.

"Oh yes, please!" I said. So I swore him to secrecy and he began to put the wheels in motion. Or so I thought. God, I was naive back then. I just took everything on trust.

One day, I called Nick from the phone box up the road and he told me that everything had been sorted with his aunt. I said I would be arriving on such and such a date and he promised to meet me at the station. When the train pulled into Euston, I found myself at the wrong end of a platform that seemed to go on forever, with two tiny girls, a suitcase and various carrier bags filled with nappies and so on to juggle. I didn't know it at the time, but this was quite a good metaphor for what lay ahead of me. Mickie was asleep in the push chair – she was only about six months old and too small to be in it really, but I had no other choice – and I had Elayna on her reins, crying. It seemed to take an eternity to get to the ticket barrier, as I kept having to put the suitcase down and rearrange everything. When I finally got to the concourse, there was nobody there.

For a long time, I just stood there, not knowing what to do – there were no mobile phones back then, of course. But eventually we found a bench and sat on it. We were there for over an hour. Eventually, Mickie woke up and started screaming. I had made up some formula for her in a small thermos and was just starting to feed her when Nick came bounding up with this Scientologist friend called Stan, who was a mad artist but a lovely guy.

"I'm so, so sorry to be late" Nick panted. Then he hit me

with it. "Look," he said, "I'm really sorry about this, but my aunt doesn't want you."

I just stared at him. Eventually I said, "What the hell am I supposed to do then?" Well, he said, I could come back with him to his mother's house, but I'd have to share his room. It turned out that Fran had gone to see her parents in America with their two little boys and had decided to stay there, so there was a vacancy in his bed. That was the deal, and there was no other offer on the table, so I accepted it.

Stan had a car and he drove us to Hampstead, where Nick's mother, Celia, had a huge house backing onto the Heath. She was a highly successful author, who wrote psychological thrillers under her maiden name Fremlin. I think she was pretty horrified when Nick arrived with a harassed-looking woman she didn't know from Adam, plus two tiny girls, and announced we had come to stay, particularly as he still theoretically had a wife. But she was wonderful to us. She said she had a cot in the attic that Mickie could use, so Nick brought it down, along with a mattress for Elayna, and put them a room at least two floors below his bedroom, where I had to sleep until he had finished with me and started snoring. Then I would go downstairs to be with the girls, sleeping rolled up in a blanket on the floor.

I was absolutely frantic about this arrangement, because my daughters were so small. He started to have sex with me that first night. I felt desperate but I wasn't in a position to argue. This went on for about a month. During that period, a Canadian girl called Mary started visiting the house increasingly often to see Nick. Then, one day he told me I needed to get out of his bed because Mary was replacing me in it. So I moved down into the room where the girls were.

This was a great relief, of course, but also ominous because I knew the situation wasn't sustainable. I must have been extremely anxious, because I remember having a turn and an ambulance coming and taking me to hospital. I presume it was some kind of panic attack. After that, Nick must have got in touch with Ian, because he pulled his finger out for once and came down to London. He got a bedsit in Dollis Hill and started looking after the girls from time to time.

Celia had been very long suffering, but eventually she presented Nick with an ultimatum. "She's got no money, I'm feeding her, and I can't keep doing it forever," she said. "She's going to have to leave." They gave me until the following Friday to make alternative arrangements. So, in desperation, I went to the local social services to ask for housing. They told me there was nothing they could do for me. Their best offer was to take the girls into care, which they said they would do if I brought them in on the day I was leaving Celia's house. I would have to fend for myself. I had no rights whatsoever, as I had left my husband voluntarily. There was a bitter irony to this, of course, because I'd been a DHSS manager while I was still in my teens, and fought for the rights of people who were up against it.

72

The one thing they did say was that I might have better luck if I went to the social services in Carlisle, because that's where my last permanent address had been. So, leaving the girls with Celia and Mary, I went up there and back in one day. I might as well not have bothered. "Because you left the area of your own volition," the housing people there said, "we're not responsible for you either. Do what they advised you to do in London. Have the girls taken into care - it's your only option." In those days, councils were not obliged to keep families together, especially those with only one parent.

I was in a very dark place indeed during the long train journey back to London. But I was sure about one thing – I was absolutely not going to let Elayna and Mickie be taken into care. So when Friday came around, I left a load of stuff at Nick's mother's house, took the girls, and we went to sleep on the streets. Or Regent's Park, to be precise.

As you can imagine, this was a total nightmare. We'd wander around all day, then head into the park to sleep. We were only there for three nights, but I can safely say it was one of the worst times in my life. Total rock bottom. I had no hope and no plan B. And I was constantly terrified that the police were going to find us and take the girls away. As far as physical comfort went, the weather was warm enough – that wasn't the problem. It was dealing with the nappies that drove me to despair. There were no disposables in those days, and Elayna, being fully weaned, was filling hers

73

pretty regularly. I'd have to go into the public loos and try to rinse them out, so I was constantly carting around two great carrier bags, one full of 'clean' nappies, the other stuffed with used ones.

By the Monday, I could stand it no longer, and decided to throw myself on Celia's mercy. She'd always been very kind to me. Surely, I told myself, she'd let me wash some nappies? So I went to her house and knocked on the door. When she opened it, she looked at me and asked what on earth I was doing there. I burst into tears, so she took me downstairs to the kitchen, made me a cup of tea, and I told her the whole story. When I'd finished, she said she couldn't promise me anything, but by amazing coincidence she'd just been speaking to a friend on the phone whose live-in cleaner had walked out on her. Now this lady, Fanny, needed a replacement, and if I was interested, she'd put me forward as a possibility.

London, Summer 1968

Riversdale Rd in London, Christmas 1968. I am four months pregnant

Not long before we left Carlisle and ran away to London

5

MAPESBURY ROAD

Please don't say you love me when you rock me in bed
I get a funny feeling inside of my head
Cos I'm just short-term accommodation
And you are just a temporary man.

— Anne Lennox-Martin, *'Temporary Man'*

I took Celia up on her offer in a heartbeat. Soon she was on the phone to her friend, telling her that I was a nice, well-educated girl who found herself in dreadful circumstances and was desperate to find a job that would allow her to keep her children with her. Fanny must have responded positively, because Celia promptly put me and the girls in a taxi and dispatched us to the Cockerells' house in Mapesbury Road, Brondesbury.

It stood on a corner and was absolutely massive, with

three floors and a cellar. Fanny invited us in and was very nice to me. She was also sweet with the girls, which I took as a good sign. She noticed that I was very nervous about her two big dogs, so, displaying a degree of sensitivity that I would later discover was highly unusual for her, she shut them up in another room while we went into the dining room for my interview.

When we were finished, she said she needed to see how I got on with cleaning a room, so she took me upstairs to a bedroom, handed me a hoover and some dusters and left me to get on with it. I sat the girls on the bed and told them not to move on pain of death. Then I cleaned that room to within an inch of its life. When Fanny came in and saw what I had done, she was very pleased and offered me the job on the spot. I'd told her during the interview that if I got it, I'd want to move in straight away, so she took me to the top of the house to show me the flat (it was actually two rooms, with shared amenities).

The first thing I noticed was that it was full of the belongings of the previous occupants. What I didn't realise yet but would soon find out was that they had been Fanny's nephew Dan and his wife. They had only just got married, and the wife had agreed to do the cleaning in return for their accommodation. But something had spooked her and they'd done a midnight flit, leaving all their possessions behind, including several unwrapped wedding presents. Purportedly, she had seen ghosts, but knowing what I do now, I suspect the real reason was that she couldn't stand working for Fanny. Mind you, my daughters always vowed that they had seen ghosts there as well, so… who knows?

Aside from all their clobber, there was hardly any furniture – just a sideboard, two single beds, an armchair and an awful old carpet. There were no sheets, so we had to borrow some from Fanny. There was a little kitchen area with a small gas oven and sink on the landing, and a long, thin bathroom tucked under the eaves, which I was told we would have to share with the ballet company that used the large studio room next to ours. There would be about 16 dancers going in and out of it all day. It wasn't the most appealing set-up I had ever seen, but it was a great deal better than Regent's Park and I thought it was a miracle.

While I was taking everything in, somebody shouted up the stairs. It was Dan's sister Naomi, who ran the ballet company with her husband and lived with him on the floor below (everything was very incestuous in that house). Fanny went down to talk to them and a blood-curdling row ensued.

"You promised us that you wouldn't have anyone with children again," I heard them screaming. "We don't want people like that above us. We are not putting up with it!" I listened on in horror. "Oh my God, Fanny," I prayed. "Don't let them change your mind. Please, please, please! You're my only hope!"

Eventually she came back upstairs, looking flustered but determined. "They don't want you here," she told me, "but

I've said it's my house and you're staying." I thanked her over and over again. Then she said she'd send her man up to help me pack up Dan and his wife's things and move them into Naomi's flat below. Needless to say, this went down with the niece like a lead balloon.

The odd job man, Tom Green, wasn't much better. He had been very close to Dan, and he laid into me something rotten. "How can you possibly do it?" he said to me. "They've only just got married! This is a young couple, these are their wedding presents, some haven't been opened yet, and here you are packing them all up!" He thought it was just awful that the family should bring someone in so quickly. I didn't blame him for his opinion, but I was so desperate.

So that was my introduction to life in Mapesbury Road. Everything felt very tenuous and chaotic, as it would for the best part of the next 15 years.

Before I go into more depth about what living there was like, I want to give you an overall picture of the house and its inhabitants.

The Cockerells were very interesting and well-connected. Fanny came from a very rich White Russian family, who had managed to get out of the country around the time of the revolution with all their cash. Her husband, Hugh (OBE) was wealthy in his own right – he was a big shot in the insurance world and went off to the City every day. In the early days, he wouldn't even talk to me, but by the time I'd been there 10 years, I'd comforted him in my arms like I did every other member of the family sooner or later.

Their eldest son, Michael, was a reporter on the current affairs programme *Panorama* and became one of the BBC's most eminent political documentary makers. He had married a granddaughter of the former Prime Minister Harold MacMillan and moved to Putney. Then there were Fanny's two grown-up children still living in the house in Mapesbury Road who were both older than me: Lolly, who was absolutely beautiful and became quite a good friend of mine, and David, who will become a very significant figure in this story. He was an electronics wizard and invented the machine that the theme tune to *Doctor Who* was played on. He was lovely to me but also very strange and withdrawn. Eventually, I discovered a possible explanation. Not long before I moved into the house, his youngest brother had committed suicide – Fanny had found him hanging in what I think was now David's room. You can only imagine what this tragedy had done to her, David, and the whole family. They didn't talk about it – in the end, Lolly told me what had happened – but it was always there in the background.

I need to explain my ambivalent feelings about Fanny in particular. I was supremely grateful to her for having taken us in, and there is no doubt that had she not done so that day, this would have been a very different story. But she was a complex character – a nightmare to deal with, but with a heart of gold that came through at unexpected moments. I grew to loathe her behaviours but love her flashes of generosity, which made it impossible for me to hate or judge her. Working for someone who was a staunch Labour supporter yet had no understanding of what it was like to be trapped in poverty and powerless to change your situation made my life in Mapesbury Road a complete misery for the first five years, and an increasing challenge for the next 10. More of that later. In the meantime, back to the house!

Working our way down, on the top floor there was me and the girls, in a room divided into two by a stud partition, plus the ballet studio. There were half floors on each landing with family bedrooms. The middle floor was occupied by Naomi and her husband, their daughter Tanya, who had a room of her own, and Lolly, who had a bedsit there. David's room, which was huge, with a full-size snooker table, was on the next floor down, as were Hugh's study and the most enormous living room. Then you went down some stairs to a sort of half-landing at ground floor level, and that's where the kitchen, bathroom and dining room were.

The most infuriating thing about the way the house was structured was that there was just the one front door for everyone. That meant that there was absolutely no privacy – to get to any of the rooms, you had to walk through the family part of the house, and anyone could just wander in anywhere if they wanted to. No one had their own entrance, as the place had never been converted from a family house, despite all the different people living and working there. The longer I was there, the more I hated not having a front door of my own. Whenever I had to leave the girls in the flat, I was constantly terrified that they would crawl out and fall down the stairs, because there was no door to stop them. Meanwhile, there were these two big dogs at large and I was terrified that they might bite the girls, especially at first, when they didn't know them. Plus, there was no fire escape, so it all felt terribly dangerous, particularly as Fanny was perpetually setting the kitchen on fire. She was an absent-minded cook, who managed to burn things like eggs and frozen peas. She'd just put something on or in the oven and then totally forget about it, until the house was full of smoke.

The result of all this was that I never dared let the girls out of my sight. This meant that I had to carry them downstairs whenever I had to go there (at least until they got big enough to walk up and down safely). And this happened all the time, because Fanny was incredibly demanding. She'd summon me by ringing the front doorbell, often on the slightest pretext, like she when she couldn't find her glasses. She also had no concept of 'time off' for me, so if she had a party, she'd think nothing of dragging me downstairs at 10 or 11 to do the dishes. The girls would be asleep in bed and I had a hook to lock them in with to prevent them coming out and hurting themselves. I grew to hate the sound of that bell, yet I'd react to it like one of Pavlov's dogs, dropping whatever I was doing, grabbing the girls if they were awake and racing downstairs to find out what she wanted. It was incessant, day and night.

Eventually, I told Fanny that I couldn't physically keep bringing these children up and down three flights of stairs all the time, especially as they were growing and getting heavier. So she agreed to put in an intercom, which at least meant that I could ask her what she wanted me to do without having to go downstairs to find out. Often, I could just say something like, "Your keys are on the kitchen table." But that intercom became a curse in its own right, because it made it so easy for Fanny to call for me at the drop of a hat.

I remember one terrible time when we all had gastroenteritis. The girls got it first, and I looked after them and carried on cleaning, but then I succumbed. I simply couldn't move. I was vomiting all the time, and it was Elayna's job – poor little thing, she could only have been about four – to empty the contents of the potty I was sick in into the loo, then rinse it and bring it back so I could fill it again for the next round. She'd always been incredibly caring – I remember bursting into tears in Carlisle and her stroking my back to comfort me when she was just nine months old – but this was a hell of a burden to put on the shoulders of such a small girl. And all the time she'd have Fanny on the intercom, asking her when I was coming down. Elayna did her best to tell her that Mummy was ill, but she wouldn't let up. Nobody came up to see how we were or to offer any kind of help the whole time I was ill.

But that was Fanny for you. As I have said, she was a real Jekyll and Hyde character. She did have a kind heart, but she could also be incredibly insensitive and callous. Of course, she must have been totally traumatised by what had happened to her youngest son, but I didn't know about that for a long time. In any case, I was so busy trying to survive that I had very little empathy or time for anybody else's hard times. I don't think Fanny's split personality can be entirely explained by the suicide, though. She had always been extremely difficult, as I would later learn from the family doctor.

The whole family could be amazingly cold. My first duty of the day was to get breakfast cooked and laid out on the table by 7.30 a.m. (they always had boiled eggs). Then I had to walk through the dining room while they were eating to start on the cleaning. Nobody would say good morning or smile or acknowledge me in any way.

It eerily reminded me of being deemed to be in a 'state of non-existence' by the Scientologists. When I got into facilities management, it was always one of my passions to raise the status of the unseen, because I knew from first-hand experience how soul-destroying it was to be treated as if you were invisible.

I absolutely hated doing the cleaning, but it was the only way of keeping a roof over our heads. One of the worst things about it was these blessed candlesticks. I thought they were gross, but Fanny absolutely adored them. They had probably belonged to her parents, and over the years, they had been cleaned so much that a lot of the silver had worn away and the base plate was coming through. No matter how hard you tried, you could never make them look like anything. But Fanny was obsessed with them. I could spend the whole morning cleaning the living room, which was huge, as I mentioned, with parquet flooring and a big rug in the middle. Then she'd come in and say, "But you haven't done the candlesticks." Everything else would be perfect, but all she would notice was those fucking candle sticks. I'm amazed I never hit her over the head with one of them.

The kitchen was dreadful too, because Fanny was so messy. She would make pastry in what she told me was the traditional Jewish way, with one pot of flour and another of used grease, both of which she'd put her hands in. What I'm sure was not traditional was not washing them before opening cupboards and so on. She'd leave finger marks of floury grease everywhere, and the outsides of the pots would be coated in coagulated layers of the stuff. There was also this disgusting dishwasher, which was never maintained and in a revolting state by the time I was using it.

The kitchen could be positively dangerous too, as could other parts of the house. One time Fanny got Tom Green, the handyman, to change over the water heater by the kitchen sink. There was no Corgi registration or gas safety regulations in those days, and of course he botched the job horribly. He took the boiler off the wall and forgot to turn off the pilot light. I remember coming down the steps to the kitchen and seeing this flame shooting out between the work surfaces and the cupboards. It just went *whoosh*. Somehow, I seemed to know instantly what I needed to do. I went to the bathroom, got a wet towel, and then sort of walked the flame back to the wall. Then Tom turned the gas off at the mains – he was a complete nightmare, but at least he had the sense to do that – and I went into shock. It was only later that I found out that the flame could have been blown or sucked back, in which case the whole house might have gone up.

Then there was the time I was almost killed while cleaning David's room... But we'll come back to that in a minute. What I want to stress for now is that for all the work I did in that house – I had to clean from 7 a.m. to 1 p.m. every day except Sunday and constantly be on call to do whatever was asked of me the rest of the time – I was paid precisely zero. Nothing. Just the roof over our heads. And for that, I was supposed to be eternally grateful, as I was continually reminded. Fanny wouldn't even give me what was called a 'Married Woman's Stamp', which would have contributed to my future pension. She said it would be taxable, and she wasn't having that. Frankly, though, I think the real reason was that she liked having me trapped. She didn't want to get involved in anything that might give me hopes of independence, even in the distant future.

Well, I *was* grateful. But I was also full of resentment. I was effectively a domestic slave, and not surprisingly, I didn't like it. All the three of us had to live on was the benefit I was entitled to claim, which was £3.95 a week plus milk vouchers. To rub salt into the wound, Fanny used to leave great wads of cash lying about the place, because she was so careless and absent-minded. I once found £200 in a wastepaper basket, which was a fortune in those days. I kept it, because I felt I'd more than earned it, but it ate away at me as I had been brought up to be very honest. Still, it lasted me for nearly two years and enabled me to buy little bits and pieces.

I used to tell the girls it was Lennox-Martin Women against the world, and that's how it felt. To eke the money out, I would cook what I called 'fuck all soup'. I'd first started making it when I was living with Ian in Riversdale Road and we had no money. I'd go to the Angel market, which was just down from Highbury, and ask the butchers for a bone for the dog, which they gave away for free on Saturday afternoons. Then I'd scavenge the market for any bruised vegetables the stallholders had discarded that still looked just about edible. When I got home, I'd make a huge pan of soup, with the bone providing the nutrients. It used to last us for a week!

So, even though we were in this great big posh house, we lived like paupers. There were rats in their kitchen and the flat upstairs was infested with mice. I found one under my pillow once and it bit my finger. I put down some mousetraps, but I was terrified that the girls would set them off and get their fingers broken. Similarly, when I eventually persuaded Fanny to get the rodent people in to do something about the rats in the kitchen, I was afraid that Elayna or Mickie would eat some of the poison.

I was constantly worried that something dreadful was going to happen to them. Everything in that house was just so unsafe. There was one episode when I found the girls crawling out onto the flat roof above their room. If I hadn't spotted them, I'm sure they would have fallen. Fortunately, I was back in touch with my father then and he fitted a grille to prevent it happening again. He also got me a fire ladder, which eased my paranoia about us burning to death up there if the gas exploded or Fanny started one of her kitchen fires. But my nerves were still permanently shredded.

I don't mean to imply there were never any fun times at Mapesbury Road, because there were. For one thing, I started having a relationship with David after I'd been there for a year or two. You wouldn't really call it an affair. We both considered ourselves single and it was an on-and-off sort of thing, which fitted with David, who was a very on-and-off sort of person. It was just sex, basically, but given that I was a highly sexed being, that was a jolly good thing from my point of view. And Fanny was absolutely delighted about it, because it meant that he wasn't homosexual, had a girlfriend of sorts and wasn't completely retreating into his shell. She and Hugh even invited me to have breakfast with them when they discovered I was sleeping in David's room at night. So my status changed in one way, yet in another it didn't change at all. I was still very much the cleaner and it all felt extremely strange. Leaving the girls on their own three floors up ate away at me, until David extended the intercom to his room.

Then there was sunbathing in the nude with Lolly on that flat roof the girls had tried to crawl on to. She used to connive with me to get me out of doing Fanny's work. "Come on, let's go up on the roof!" she'd say. It felt like bunking off school. I remember doing it a lot during the famously hot summer of 1976, when I was permanently nut-brown. The police helicopters used to spot us and zoom in close to get a better look, waving and blowing kisses at us. I can't say I blame them, because Lolly was stunning and I was pretty hot stuff back then too, if I say so myself. I distinctly remember thinking "What a waste," because I wasn't in a relationship at the time and hadn't been for quite a while.

Another time, Fanny got herself a kitten. One day she lost it and called me downstairs to help look for it, but to no avail. When I went back upstairs, I saw the girls coming out of the toilet. They were smiling, with that look on their faces that children have when they've been up to something.

"What are you doing?" I asked them.

"We was just teaching him to thwim, Mummy," Elayna said. So I opened the toilet door and this poor cat came streaking out and fled down the stairs.

So there were moments of sunlight, but for the most part, this was a dark, dark period for me. It wasn't just the poverty or the danger or the awful sense of being trapped in a situation that I was convinced was not where I was supposed to be. What made it all so difficult was that, as well as being terrifically demanding, Fanny could be overwhelmingly kind. She adored my girls and would take them on trips to the zoo and the park and so on. Part of me was grateful to her for this, of course, but I found it terrifying, because she was a dreadful driver, and there were no seatbelts or child seats back then. I also bitterly resented the fact that she was out there having fun with Elayna and Mickie, providing them with the kind of experiences that I felt I, as their mother, should be giving them, while I was stuck in the house doing the cleaning. It was similar when their birthdays came around. The Cockerells would buy them very expensive presents, while I hardly had the money to get them anything at all. It felt like my family was being taken away from me, and all the time, I was expected to show my gratitude.

Nowadays, I suppose they'd describe what Fanny was doing as a form of gaslighting. Was she my friend and saviour or a tyrant imprisoning me and trying to steal my children from under my nose? Well, she was both. I'm not saying she did it deliberately – I'm sure it was unconscious – but her behaviour kept me in a permanent state of fear, uncertainty and dependence. There was never a moment's peace and I cried myself to sleep every night. Eventually, living with her started to take a serious toll on my mental and physical health.

I don't know if it was a stress reaction, an allergy to certain cleaning materials or what, but at one stage, the skin started coming off my hands in strips. I was so overwrought that one day I did something terrible. In a fit of temper, I threw Elayna across the bedroom and she landed up against the wall. This was one of the worst things I have ever done, and it frightened me. So I made an appointment to see the Cockerell's family doctor. He was old-school and brusque, but he was wonderful to me. "You've got to have a week where you are not doing any cleaning and don't have the children," he told me. "I need to put emollients on your hands and bandage them, and I will visit you at home every day. You can't go on like this." Doctor Naschen knew exactly what Fanny was like and he loathed her. I tried to tell him about her nice side but he wasn't having any of it.

By this time, I was back in touch with my sister, who offered to have the girls for a week, so David drove them to her house in his Jag. I then had a week of precious rest. Fanny didn't like this one bit, but she had to accept it because the doctor had spoken to her. She never came to see me though. She left me alone for a few days, then on the Saturday she asked me when I was going to start cleaning again. No "How are you?" or anything like that.

Before long, I was back at Dr Naschen's again because I was haemorrhaging badly – I'd always had bad periods. This time, he told me bluntly to get out of Mapesbury Road. He said he had been looking after Fanny's cleaners for years, and that I would never be right while I carried on living with her. But I told him I had nowhere else to go.

The next medical emergency was Elayna having a terrible asthma attack. She'd suffered from the condition from a very young age, but this was much worse than usual. I remember rushing her up to the surgery – we still didn't have a phone – and coming back to Mapesbury Road absolutely at the end of my tether. I had to carry both girls up the stairs, and as I passed Naomi's room, she came out and said to me, with withering contempt, "Just look at you. I could feel sorry for you if you weren't so sorry for yourself."

The awful thing is that she was right. I did feel very, very sorry for myself and was probably clinically depressed by then. I wasn't eligible for housing, because I already had accommodation as part of my unpaid job, and I just saw no way out. I couldn't see any light at the end of the tunnel. In fact, I couldn't even find a tunnel.

Then something happened that brought things to a head – the incident when I was nearly killed in David's room. This was life-changing for me. It happened during one of our 'off' phases. As I said before, he was this wild electronics guy, and he had this upright device in his room that had all kinds of things plugged into it. I went in there one day determined to give the place a really good clean because Fanny had been complaining about what a bad cleaner I was, and I didn't want to lose my job. So I decided to move the glorified extension lead or whatever it was in order to get proper access to the carpet. I reached around it to get a decent grip, and my left hand clamped against a plug that had no back on it, so all the live wiring was exposed. The next thing I knew, I was thrown violently across the room. I must have been between the bed and the snooker table, because I didn't hit anything until I reached the wall. I remember sliding down it and hearing somebody screaming. It turned out to be me.

I crawled out of the bedroom like a wounded rabbit, and Fanny came running up to me asking what on earth the matter was. I couldn't speak, because my jaw had started to lock by this time, but I managed to mime that somebody had to fetch the girls from school. Then she called an ambulance, which took me to hospital with blue lights flashing. There was an awful kerfuffle when I arrived, because apparently my heart had stopped. They put something in my arm, possibly adrenaline, to get it started again, then they took me to A&E.

I was there until 11 p.m., by which time they had stabilised me. I told them that I urgently had to get home to the girls, as there was nobody to look after them. They said, "Ok, you might as well go home, but you have concussion, because your brain rocked in your head when you received the electric shock." Actually, they explained, it would have killed me if I hadn't been dusting beforehand. As a result, there was no moisture on my left hand. If there had been, apparently my other hand would automatically have clamped onto the machine as well, completing the circuit, and the charge would have gone through my heart for an extended period and finished me off. As it was, the shock only went through my body momentarily and I was thrown across the room.

When I got back to Mapesbury Road, I told Fanny that I would not be cleaning David's room again until he'd sorted out the electrics. You'd think that was pretty reasonable, but that wasn't Fanny's attitude. At first, she supported me and nagged David to fix the problem, but in less than a week, when nothing had been done about it, she reverted to demanding mode. She kept on at me about it for weeks. "Come on, come on, you can do his room," she kept on saying. The insensitivity of it was incredible. Then one day, she got really angry with me for refusing, and I became absolutely enraged. As people say, a black mist descended and I totally lost it with her. I very nearly strangled her and I'm not joking. My hands were going for her throat when I pulled back from the brink. I don't know which one of us was more shocked. But instead of murdering her, I banged on the table with my fists and ran out of the room in tears. She could easily have thrown me out at that stage, and with justification, but I think she realised she had pushed me too far and was sorry.

By this time, I was doing some part time cleaning at the Cricklewood branch of EMS (Electronic Music Studios), the synthesizer company David ran with his partner Peter

Zinovieff. This affected my benefits, so once childcare costs were taken into account, I only had 50p extra, but it gave me back some self-respect and that was priceless. I'll tell you more about working there in the music chapter, but the relevance of the job for now is that's where I headed after my row with Fanny. There was this sweet guy called Richard there, and he was very supportive. By the time I had told him the whole story, he was ready to go to the house and murder her himself!

Anyway, I calmed down enough to collect Mickie from the nursery I used to leave her at while I cleaned the studio, but I was still in a terrible state. That night, after I had put the children to bed, I remember sitting there listening to the record player my sister had given me, wondering how I was going to stop myself from killing this woman. "I have got to do something differently," I decided, "because if I carry on like this, I am going to end up in prison. I'll lose my girls and they will lose me. I've got to find a way of getting some control." (Elayna will tell you that her early memories of me are that I had no control of my emotions whatsoever. It was absolutely true, until that night.)

Suddenly, when I needed it most, I had a moment of inspiration. I realised that I couldn't change Fanny, but I could change the way I dealt with her and treated her. I had no knowledge of psychology, but I decided that I was going to start treating her as a very dear friend. So that's what I did. Within a month, she had started to change. By the time

I had been doing it for a year, she had begun to see me as like a daughter. Then I started using the same approach with Hugh. It worked like a charm and David was very supportive, because he saw how hard I was trying with his parents. I think he was really in love with me, but he didn't know how to show it because he was so introverted. Our sexual relationship was on and off with no real explanation.

From that day on, I stopped being angry because I had taken back control. Before that, life had been a constant battle – I had been against everyone and everything. Now my relationships began to improve. I have used that tactic of treating difficult people as if they are just having a bad day ever since, in both my personal and professional life. What I have found is that when you see the good in people, they'll give you the good back.

Fanny Cockerell sitting on the stairs at Mapesbury Rd, 1970s (probably)

David Cockerell, a lovely man!

Myself and Lolly Cockerell around 1973/1974 in my mother's garden

6

POLITICS:
TALKING THE WALK I'D WALKED

Just because I need a private space
Don't mean I'm entitled to a permanent place.
— Anne Lennox-Martin, *'Temporary Man'*

'd always been a political animal, and the one aspect of living at Mapesbury Road that was unquestionably good from my point of view was the access it gave me to the world of politics. Fanny was a leading light in the Labour Party, and very instrumental in getting Ken Livingstone deselected as MP for Brent, which I remember vividly, because he was very cross about it. She was also a long-standing member of the Progressive League, which was an organisation founded in 1932 by H.G. Wells and C.E.M Joad. It stood for a lot of the things I believed in, like reform of the divorce laws and the legalisation of abortion and homosexuality, many of which had already happened to some extent by the time I got involved.

For 25 years, Fanny edited The Progressive League's magazine, which was called *Plan: For Freedom and Progress*. She was quite a good writer in her own way, and I used to help out, contributing articles and other bits and pieces, which did wonders for my self-confidence. I also met all sorts of fascinating people as a result of Fanny's political activities. Mapesbury Road was one of the nerve centres of what some people called 'the Hampstead set', and lots of the great and good from the left end of the spectrum were in and out of the house, like Reg Freeson, who was twice Minister for Housing under Labour; Hugh Jenkins, who was Arts Minister and later Chair of CND; the novelist Margaret Drabble; and the playwright Arnold Wesker.

Of course, Fanny being herself, her left-wing political views were very Fanny-ish. By that I mean they were theoretical rather than practical. She had no empathy whatsoever for people in poverty. Whenever there were strikes (and there were a lot of them in that era, particularly during the winter of 1973-4 when Edward Heath introduced the three-day week), her attitude would be, "How dare they?" She'd be slagging off the dustmen or whoever and I'd say, "Fanny, you're supposed to be Labour aren't you?" Meanwhile, she had a real-life example of a worker being exploited by the forces of capitalism living under her roof – me! – and she was the one doing the exploiting. As I mentioned before, she wouldn't even give me a Married Woman's Stamp. But the contradictions seemed to pass over her head completely. What mattered above all was whether or not Fanny was being inconvenienced. It was classic 'champagne socialism', really. She genuinely had strongly held principles, but she didn't always find it easy to apply them in her personal life.

Fanny did have a kind heart, though, mixed in with all the other stuff. One of the ways she showed it was by taking me and the girls on holidays to Beatrice Webb House in Dorking, where the Progressive League held summer schools. I was still at Fanny's beck and call while we there, but I got to meet all these good-hearted people, which was magical for me, and the girls got to do things like art classes and country dancing, which they adored. Afterwards, Fanny started taking them to dance lessons in Conway Hall in Red Lion Square in Holborn. She was interested in the English Folk Dance and Song Society, and did quite a lot of dancing herself. In fact, it was partly through her that I got involved in the folk scene, and she was always very encouraging about my music, for which I'm genuinely grateful.

Fanny also helped me out with advice when it came to getting divorced from Ian, which I did around 1973. Unfortunately, she was so remote from the 'real' world that it ended up costing me much more than it should have. She recommended a smart lawyer for me, who I had to pay out of my hard-earned wages from cleaning David's music studio. I ended up having to go to the Old Bailey to get the divorce, and later found out that I could have got it much cheaper. But that was Fanny for you. Afterwards, David took us all out for a meal to celebrate, so this must have been during one of our 'on' periods.

Many of the things the Progressive League campaigned for were very close to my heart, like proper help for single-parent families and equal tax regimes for men and women. The thing that really changed my life, though, was meeting Margaret Bramall at Mapesbury Road. She was a smoker, thank God, otherwise it might never have happened. One evening in what must have been 1973, Fanny called me on the intercom and summoned me downstairs to wash up some glasses. She used to do this kind of thing a lot when she had people round – sometimes she would even get me to serve drinks to her guests to make herself look important. Anyway, there I was slaving away at the sink, when this woman came down the small flight of stairs from the living room and popped into the garden for a cigarette. On her way back, she saw me scrubbing away and stopped to have a chat. I had no idea who she was, but she was lovely and asked me all sorts of questions. I told her I was a single parent employed by Fanny to do the cleaning and so on.

At the end of our conversation, she said, "Do you know what? I think you are the most articulate person in your situation I've ever met." This was a wonderful thing for me to hear, as it was the first affirmation I'd had in a very long time. It turned out that Margaret was the director of the National Council for One Parent Families (NCOPF), or as it was then known, the National Council for the Unmarried Mother and Her Child. In other words, she was in charge of the most prominent organisation in the country dedicated to people in my position!

At this point, I could almost see a lightbulb going off in her head. She told me that the Council was just in the process of changing its name and the way it was run. They wanted to make it less 'patrician' and more suited to what life was really like for people on benefits. I, as someone who was in exactly the kind of predicament they were campaigning about, would make a perfect spokesperson. I wouldn't just be some worthy do-gooder talking about the issues – I'd lived them! "Would you like to get involved?" she asked me. "It would be great to have you on the management board. We meet up in Camden Town Hall in Judd Street near King's Cross."

I was completely bowled over. "Oh my God, that sounds so interesting," I told her. "But I don't have any money and I've got these two little children to look after, so I don't see how I could get to the meetings."

"What would you say if we could find a way around that?" she asked me.

"In that case, I'd absolutely love to," I said. And find a way around it they did. They gave me travel vouchers and even altered the times of their meetings so I could bring the girls with me. Elayna and Mickie would sit on the floor with their colouring-in books while we adults addressed the plight of single parents across the land!

Getting me on the board was a very far-sighted and progressive thing for Margaret to do. The first time I went to Judd Street, I was very intimidated – it was all 'Bishop this' and 'Lady that', sitting around a table with silver teapots. I was just a cleaning lady and there was no one else like me there. For the first two or three times I was very quiet. But Margaret would come to the house afterwards to talk about what had been discussed in the meetings and ask me for my thoughts on them, which helped boost my confidence. I can't tell you how affirming it was to have my opinions valued like that. I started to become more assertive at the meetings, and before long, the Council asked me to front this publicity campaign they were doing about the name change. Suddenly, I found myself appearing on all kinds of radio and TV shows, which was wonderful. But I couldn't accept any payment, or I would have lost my benefits. So all the money I would have earned went to the charity. In return, the Council arranged for me to go on a holiday with Gingerbread.

This was an era when all kinds of grassroots organisations were setting themselves up, and Gingerbread grew into one of the best known of them. It was a self-help group for single parents, founded in 1970 by a wonderful lady called Tessa Fothergill, who Margaret had put me in touch with. I used to go to a few of their meetings in the early days. Eventually, in 2007, the two organisations merged, and the NCOPF became part of Gingerbread.

So off I went with the girls and my mother to a holiday camp somewhere in the West Country. A whole week of swimming pool and sunshine, with everything paid for! They even gave me some spending money! I'd never really been on holiday before – I wouldn't put going to Beatrice Webb house with Fanny in that category, because I'd still been 'on duty' there, nor those dismal trips to Troon with my parents – so it was a wonderful experience for me. I even got up and sang at one point – there's a picture of me there with a guitar. I hadn't done that for ages.

Given what had come before, you may be surprised to hear that my mother came too, but our relationship had defrosted somewhat. As I mentioned, she'd sneaked off to see me sometimes when I was living in Highbury with Ian, and she'd even come to Elayna's christening, telling my father she was going to Scotland to visit her parents. Then, about a year before the holiday, he had told her he was leaving her. At first, according to my sister, she had been absolutely suicidal. She had no idea how to cope on her own and was beside herself. I had no sympathy for her – I was working 7 a.m. to 5 p.m. every day, so my life wasn't exactly a bed of roses either, plus she'd never shown much compassion for me. But since then, she'd got herself a part time job, so at least she was making an effort. Then a miracle had happened: Wendy's father had proposed to her! She was as giddy as a schoolgirl during that holiday and kept asking me if she should accept or not.

I wouldn't say I'd forgiven her for slapping me when I'd told her about my grandfather or putting the phone down on me when I was in that desperate state in Carlisle, but I could never have been horrible to her face. She was just too vulnerable for that. And both our lives were on the up by this stage, so I didn't want to rock the boat. To give my mother her due, she did enter the spirit of the holiday, even entering the 'Glamorous Granny' contest. She didn't come first, but the girls did win the fancy dress competition in outfits she'd made for them, and danced in long skirts I'd sewn for them from some cheap material I'd bought at the market.

All good things come to an end, and before I knew it, I was back in London working as Fanny's skivvy. But things were different now. A glimpse of light had appeared at the end of the tunnel as a result of my involvement in the NCOPF. It started to burn even brighter in July 1974, when the Finer Report came out. This was the result of a royal commission into the problems facing one-parent families, and it was a very big deal for the Council, as we were responsible for most of the 230 recommendations in the document.

I got an opportunity to get even more heavily involved when the NCOPF invited me to join the fundraising and grants committees. Then, after the Finer Report came out, I started being invited to appear on more and more TV and radio shows. I also began to interact directly with prominent politicians and bodies like the Finer Report Joint Action Committee. My life became a whirl of media interviews and meetings with the great and the good.

To give you an idea of the kind of circles I suddenly found myself moving in, the grants committee used to meet in the offices of one of the members in Threadneedle Street in the City, where the Bank of England is. When I saw the sandwiches they'd laid on for us, my eyes were out on stalks. "I don't think you've got any idea of what it's like to be a single parent reliant on benefits," I said to all these heavyweight financial people. "This food could feed me and my family for a week. Can I have a doggy bag?"

I was completely fearless, whoever I was dealing with, because we were Lennox-Martin women against the world. At last we had a voice, and we were damned well going to use it. I remember going to see Harry Shepherd, the chief executive of Marks & Spencer, at his office in Baker Street to meet with his fundraising guy. His secretary must have thought I wasn't being deferential enough, because she said to me, "Do you not realise who you are going to see?"

"I don't care who he is," I told her. "I'm here to get the right treatment for one-parent families and I need to explain what it's like."

Then there was the man who ran the Playboy Club. He had been a strong supporter of the NCOPF since the 'Unmarried Mother and Her Child' days and chaired the fundraising committee. I took the girls to a meeting he had set up at the Playboy Club once. We shared a lift with one of the Bunny Girls, and Mickie started stroking her tail. It was hilarious!

One day, I went to the Houses of Parliament with Harry Shepherd to talk to Barbara Castle about the implementation of the Finer Report (which never really happened in the end, though we definitely made progress). She was the Secretary of State for Health and Social Services at the time, and a right old battleaxe. I didn't like her at all – she reminded me of my mother a bit, with her old-fashioned 'Well you've made your bed so you'd better lie in it' attitude.

"There are far more deserving cases than one-parent families that I need to think about," she told me. I freely admitted that there were lots of things that needed sorting out in terms of equality and justice, but child poverty was a huge issue which deserved consideration. Lots of her Labour colleagues agreed with me, like Frank Field from the Child Poverty Action Group and Patricia Hewitt from the National Council for Civil Liberties. So Barbara Castle and I had this big argument.

Although we didn't agree, I think she must have been quite impressed by me, because not long afterwards she got some of her officials to ask me to join a government working group that was developing new pamphlets for the parents of children who had been taken into care. This, of course, had nearly happened to my own children, so it was an issue I felt very strongly about. The existing pamphlets were a complete nonsense, written by toffee-nosed idiots who didn't know what ordinary people's language was. When I read them, I thought, "I'm reasonably articulate and well-educated and I don't understand them, so what chance does the average person in this predicament have with them?" One of my strengths throughout my working life has been the ability to put things in a way people can relate to, and I thought, "I can do a lot better than this." I had also done quite a lot of work with Tess and Gingerbread, and met a lot of one-parent families through the grants committee by this time, so I had quite a broad understanding of the issues. Plus, I was a very fast and hungry learner. So I helped produce some really good, easy-to-read pamphlets that explained to parents what their rights were when their children were taken into care, what they needed to be aware of and what their next steps were. I was very proud of the work I did on that group. It was yet more affirmation.

I met so many fascinating and wonderful people through NCOPF, like Erin Pizzey, who had started the world's first shelter for the victims of domestic abuse in Chiswick in 1971, which later became known as Refuge (obviously there was a lot of crossover between the work they did and single-parent families). But I think what I enjoyed most were the radio and TV appearances, because I've always been a performer at heart.

I did so many that I started to lose count. On the radio

side, I did the Jimmy Young Show on Radio 2, which had a huge audience, and five or six others. But the really big one was *The World at One* with William Hardcastle on Radio 4. This was serious stuff. Still the BBC's flagship news show, it describes itself as "Britain's leading political programme," going on to say, "With a reputation for rigorous and original investigation, it is required listening in Westminster." First you'd have the news headlines, then Bill would conduct in-depth interviews about the leading issues of the day. In this case with me!

I was just as busy on TV. I was on a Thames Television show called *Lone Parents*, which was just me talking to Jenny Conway, who was quite a celebrity back then and did a lot of programmes about women's issues. Then I did *Citizens' Rights* on ATV, which I wrote a song for – I wish I had a video of it, but I didn't even get to see it. I was also on *Pebble Mill at One*, a cross between a current affairs programme and a chat show which was mandatory viewing in the 70s and 80s for anyone who was stuck at home in the middle of the day. But the biggest thing I did was *Newsday* in October 1975, with Ludovic Kennedy, who was the Jeremy Paxman of the era.

To give you an idea of the stature of the programme, the other guests when I was on were Henry Kissinger and some Arab Sheikh talking about the oil crisis. And they sent a limousine to collect me! I mean, can you imagine? There's me, a cleaner on benefits, with two small girls, looking down from the top of the house and seeing this limo arrive for me. The girls were thrilled to bits. I felt on top of the world when I stepped into that car, with all the neighbours looking on.

When I got to the BBC Lime Grove Studios, they took me to the green room, where a researcher came to prepare me for my interview. He or she – I can't remember which – had a list of the questions Mr Kennedy was going to ask me, and got me to talk through what my answers were likely to be. If I said something they thought wouldn't be appropriate, they'd say, "No, don't go there, because that would probably be repetitious" or whatever. They also plied me with alcohol, which helped calm me down. The BBC were great like that, which was why so many people went on TV pissed as farts back then. Then I had my make-up done. But I was still a bit nervous when I walked out into the studio, because I was afraid they would find me stupid. Ludovic Kennedy shook my hand, like Hughie Green had a few years before, then we launched straight into the interview. It was just me, him and the cameraman, for about 10 minutes.

It turned out that I needn't have been so nervous, because it all went well. The BBC sent me a nice letter afterwards, saying, "A long overdue thank you for the interview you did with Ludovic Kennedy last month. We thought you put over the problems facing one-parent families in a very clear and lively way, and I hope you too felt it was worthwhile. I realise 10 minutes is all too short a time, even though generous by television standards!" Then they wished me all the best for success in my campaign.

When the filming was over, the limousine drove me back to Mapesbury Road. I was a television personality now, but I was still also a bloody unpaid cleaner!

Photo taken by the Sunday Mirror for their article on us

My mother in the glamorous 'grandma competition at the Gingerbread holiday

Elayna and Mickie winning 1st prize on the Gingerbread Holiday

21st November 1975

Dear Anne,

A long overdue note to thank you for the interview you did with Ludovic Kennedy towards the end of last month — we were very grateful to you, especially as the programme was confirmed at such short notice.

We thought you put over the problems facing One-Parent Families in a very clear and lively way, and I hope you too felt it was worth while. I realise ten minutes is all too short a time, even though generous by television standards!

With all good wishes for success in your campaign,

Yours sincerely,

Jennifer Davies

(Jennifer Davies)
"Newsday"

Mrs. Anne Lennox-Martin,
22 Mapesbury Road,
London, N.W.2.

7

MUSIC

If music be the food of love, play on;
— William Shakespeare, *Twelfth Night*

You may be wondering how and why my involvement in politics came to an end. It all happened pretty abruptly, during the long hot summer of 1976. The short answer is 'music'. The slightly longer one is that I met Sam, the man who ended up becoming my second husband.

We need to rewind a bit first though. By the time I had been living at Mapesbury Road for a few years, *Opportunity Knocks* and the gigs in the Scottish Borders seemed a lifetime ago, but as you will have picked up in the last couple of chapters, music had gradually started to creep back into my life. First there had been the exposure to the English Folk

Dance and Song Society through Fanny's involvement; then there was cleaning David's music studio.

The synthesisers EMS made were in hot demand, and there were all kinds of Prog Rock bands coming in and out while I was working there, like Hawkwind, Pink Floyd and Tangerine Dream. My daily routine was cleaning for Fanny until 1 p.m., then I would walk up to Cricklewood and leave Mickie at her nursery for the afternoon. When I'd finished at EMS, I would pick her up, then we'd go to Willesden Green to collect Elayna from this girl I paid to look after her after school. When we got home, I'd cook the girls their tea, then we'd all sit and watch *Crossroads* together.

After a while, in addition to the cleaning, David got me doing procurements for him. I would research and source things like transistors, resistors and electronic gates, and I turned out to be really good at it. With hindsight, perhaps this was an early sign of the talents that would serve me so well in my career in FM. I used to get special deals for David, and he started paying me a little more money as a result.

I became really interested in what the guys were doing at the studio, even though they were introverted IT types. And working there did wonders for my self-esteem. When David and I were going through one of our 'off' periods, I had a fling with Tim, who was one of the engineers and a young virgin! Graham, who did the maintenance for the bands, was very keen, and Richard, the sweet guy who calmed me down that time when I wanted to kill Fanny, was absolutely besotted with me. I think I exuded a certain *joie de vie* – I was pretty hot stuff in those days, and always toasty brown from those roof-top sunbathing sessions with Lolly.

David and I continued our on-off relationship, and as he was a kind man, once a week he offered to keep an eye on the girls after they had gone to bed so I could go out. I was earning a little bit of money now that I was cleaning his office, so I'd head for the Marquis of Clanricarde pub in Paddington, which was where the BBC folk club used to meet up. I went by the number 16 bus. I'd really been bitten by the folk bug, so this was right up my street. I used to sit nursing the one half-pint of lager I could afford, listening to the music. One evening, a shy, rather awkward little man who had noticed me on my own came over to me and offered to buy me a drink. I refused, because I couldn't buy him one back, but we got talking. His name was Alan and he was a bit of a loner. We became good friends, and eventually, after a long time, we moved on to being lovers. It just seemed like the right thing to do. But to complicate matters, by that stage I was back 'on' with David again. Then I found out I was pregnant, and I didn't know which one the father was. I felt completely torn and agonised about what to do next.

When I went to see Dr Naschen, I told him I couldn't go through with the pregnancy as I was scarcely able to manage with the two children I had already. He reluctantly agreed to put me forward for an abortion, which had only just become legal. But I didn't feel able to tell Fanny, even though she was very pro-choice. In fact, before this happened, I had met the woman who ran the national abortion movement through her, and gone on some of their marches. But I was scared of losing my job if she found out, because this could have been her first grandchild. I came clean to David and Alan, because I felt I owed it to them to be upfront about what had happened and what I was planning to do and why, but apart from them, the only other person I told was Lolly. She was the one who took me to the hospital. My father came to visit me there, but he thought I was just having a cyst removed. The nurses were dreadful to me, because I was in the same ward as women who had lost their babies or had stillbirths, and I was doing this voluntarily. I understood but it just added to my feelings of despair. When I left, one of them said, "We'll be seeing you again."

"Absolutely not," I replied.

"Oh yes we will," she said. "Your sort always comes back."

There were no hard feelings between David and me, and it wasn't long before he was volunteering to babysit for me again so I could go to the folk club at the Marquis of Clanricarde. I started doing a bit of singing there and I also began to make friends, like these guys Dave and Mike – the three of us became a bit of a triumvirate. I never had sex with either of them: we were just good pals. Then I started to go out with a guy called Derek, who I met at the club. I wasn't particularly fond of him, but he had a Jaguar E6 and

I needed a bit of a jolly. Meanwhile, he got sex, so that kept both of us happy for a while.

It was different with Sam. I lusted after him and he had no chance, really. I first got to know him because he had a 'floor spot' at the pub. That was how folk clubs worked: the regulars would get up and do their floor spots, then there would be a guest spot, then an interval. The second half would follow the same pattern. Sam had a big crowd of friends at the club, and I sort of got absorbed into them.

For a while, I was able to combine my political activities with my music. I got the BBC Folk Club involved with the One Parent Families campaign, and we did a fundraising event in Kilburn Grange Park as part of the first World Folk Day. This must have been in about May 1976. It was absolutely brilliant in itself, but a disaster in terms of raising money. We had marquees donated by Harry Shepherd at Marks & Spencer, and a load of Bunny Girls arrived in a limousine to meet the crowds, only there weren't any crowds because NCOPF had failed to market the event properly. But from a personal perspective it was a great success, and organising it led me to get to know Celia O'Neil and David Ellis, who ran the folk club. To help me improve my performance, Celia took me to Putney to meet a friend of hers called Theo-something who had a studio there. He was quite well known at the time, and a bit of an old groper, but he gave me some good advice – he told me that I had a great voice but my material was dreadful. I was still singing 60s stuff, and he advised me to listen to people like John Denver and John Martin.

Celia then suggested I join forces with Sam to play at another event that was in the pipeline. The BBC Folk Club were going to collaborate with other London clubs and take over a space in Fitzroy Square, where there would be a string of floor spots all day long, celebrating the world of folk. Sam was a brilliant guitarist but not much of a singer, while I was an excellent singer but not much of a guitarist, so we made a very good team. I started learning new songs and working with him to develop the chord structures and so on. He was very good-looking, and I became quite besotted with him. He wasn't the most articulate person in the world though, bless him. He would ring me up on, say, the Thursday, and it would be like, "Um... um, um... I was wondering... um, um, um..." Eventually, I would interject something like, "Are you saying that we should meet up?" Then he'd go back to the ums again. I'd be thinking "Oh God, dear me." I really wanted to have a relationship as I was very lonely still. We started going out together, and I think we fell for each other quite quickly. I was at my peak then, I reckon.

Sam was working on the London Underground at the time, but he originally came from the West Country. After we'd only been going out for a couple of months, he took me down to Plympton in Devon to meet his parents, which was practically unheard of back then. We drove down in his little Morris Minor, which we called 'Winnie', after Winnie-the-Pooh. I adored his parents! They had their toilet paper the 'other' way round, which I thought was the most exotic thing I'd ever seen. And they took us to the pub – parents, going to the pub!

Sam was always great with the girls. He helped bring them up and they came to regard him as their father. This was really important, as Ian had disappeared from our lives quite early on. When I'd first moved into Fanny's, he'd come to see them a couple of times after moving to that bedsit in Dollis Hill, but then he became very unreliable. I'd have them all dressed up and ready to go and he just wouldn't turn up. I remember Elayna banging her head against the wall saying, "My daddy doesn't love me," which was heartbreaking. I put a stop to it after that and told him he couldn't see the children anymore if he was going to be so unreliable.

So Sam was a godsend as far as the girls were concerned, and he and I were very close. We had a very good sexual relationship, and I was always totally faithful to him, until it all started falling apart. Very quickly, our music started taking off in a big way. We got a residency at Dingle's Folk Club in Tottenham Court Road, which was run by Roger and Helen Holt and had performers like John Kirkpatrick and Chris Foster as residents – legends on the folk scene even then. Then we did our first paid gig at Christchurch on the coast and the people down there immediately asked us to perform at their folk festival. We found ourselves becoming popular almost overnight.

Prior to this, I had been devoting all my life (apart from cleaning Fanny's house) to politics, and feeling like I was really getting somewhere with that. But it quickly became apparent that there was no way I could keep that up as well as doing the music, at least not if I was going to be any kind of mother to the girls. So I had a decision to make, and I chose Sam and the music.

There was a big backlash against American folk at the time, led by Ewan MacColl and Peggy Seeger. Instead, it was all about traditional folk music – that's what you had to sing if you wanted to get anywhere. Sam and I did a lot of research, coming up with new arrangements for traditional tunes and songs. Then we realised we needed a really great, rousing chorus song to perform at the end of our gigs to get everyone going. And that's when I remembered what I used to sing in the sandpit in Dartford when I was I little girl – all those old music hall songs that Auntie Irene down the road used to play on her piano. I did a bit of digging and found the words to *Joshua,* which became our sort of anthem:

Joshua, Joshua,
Why don't you call and see Mama?
She'll be pleased to know
You are my best beau.
Joshua, Joshua,
Nicer than lemon squash, you are.
Yes, by gosh you are,
Josh-u-osh-u-ah!

Music hall was very popular at the time. Up to 10 million people used to watch *The Good Old Days* on the BBC, which featured Victorian and Edwardian music hall songs and sketches and audiences dressed in period costume. We started to incorporate more and more music hall into our sets, until most of our songs were in that style. I had this hat that I'd bought at Camden Lock, with earrings and feather boas going down to my knees and all the rest of it. I was remarkably good at it, because I had this exhibitionist side, and it was very performative and innuendo-ey. This was the era of Benny Hill and *Are You Being Served?*, remember. It started eating at me in the end, because it reminded me too much of the abuse, and I found it difficult to balance the feminist, political part of myself with the twee, music hall dolly bird stuff. But that's what brought in the money.

I was never actually on *The Good Old Days*, but I did perform music hall on television, and I did a lot of folk broadcasts on Radio 2. I was twice on *Pick Of The Week* in fact. And I did some stuff with Richard Digance, who had his own show on Capital Radio. He loved our music hall stuff, and got us to do the Theatre Royal in Stratford, which was one of the old-time venues. That was absolutely fabulous.

We made two albums, *The Pretty Ploughboy* (1979) and *Turn The Music On* (1983), plus a Music Hall EP called *Don't Dilly Dally* (1981), which all did really well and made us a bit of money. You can still get them online. I can't imagine for a minute that anybody much buys them, but they are being advertised for what seem like incredible sums to me, because they are quite rare now. We also played the backing music on a lot of other people's records. We nearly got to do it on Fiddler's Dram's *Day Trip To Bangor (Didn't We Have A Lovely Time)*, which would have been nice as it got to number three in the UK singles chart in 1979. The band members were all great friends of ours and used to sleep on the floor at Mapesbury Road. We got them their contract at the record company, in fact.

We had so much fun doing the singing during those years, because the folk world was like one, big happy family. Everybody kissed and hugged, we drank, we made music, we laughed, and we did all sorts of mad silly things like synchronised swimming on the floor. I also got involved in something called 'Molly dancing', which is a form of morris dancing specific to Plough Monday, the first Monday after the New Year, when historically farmers would plough their fields.

To give you a flavour of what the folk scene was like back then and the kind of crazy escapades we got up to, I'll tell you the story of what I call The Worst Gig in the World. It must have happened in 1979 or 1980. We had a friend called Dave Walters, who was a very talented guy and quite famous around that time for an album he'd made based on *Songs of Innocence and Experience* by William Blake. We were all booked in to perform at the Cardiff Folk Festival together, so Dave came to the house and he, Sam, the two girls and I piled into our Morris Minor Estate, with its wooden frame, and set off for Wales. No sooner had we got onto the M4 than we had a tyre blowout. There was no spare, so I stood by the side of the road, hitched up my skirt and blagged us a lift in no time. Some very nice people drove me and Dave to a service station, where we got the wheel mended. Then we hitched back in the opposite direction. When we were dropped off parallel to where the car was, we had to trundle the wheel across six lanes of motorway, which was very nerve-racking! Anyway, the guys managed to get it back on the car and we resumed our journey. But all this had delayed us several hours, and we were due to be performing on a live radio show.

By the time we got to Cardiff, it was getting perilously close to the time when we were meant to go on stage. We didn't know the address of the venue, so we pulled up outside the civic building, where the tickets for the festival were issued, and Dave rushed up the stairs to find out where we were meant to be playing. Only he was in such a hurry that he tripped and broke his ankle. That obviously put paid to his chances of performing, so while he went to hospital, Sam and I found someone to look after the girls – there were loads of folk people we knew who were in town for the festival, so this wasn't a problem – and headed off to the gig. Where we performed to great acclaim, I don't mind telling you.

When it was over, we picked Dave up from the hospital. He was on crutches with his leg all bound up, so he was pretty fed up and positively hurled his spare shoe (the one he could no longer wear) into the back of the Morris. Then we drove to the pub where we were being put up (along with a lot of other people who were performing at the festival) by this fantastic gay couple who owned the place. They had us all playing music until about three in the morning.

We had a very nice breakfast the following morning, after which we were due to go to a 10 o'clock workshop to talk about music and develop new material. But when we left to get in the car, we found that someone had stolen it. Thankfully, we still had Sam's guitar, as he always made a point of taking it into wherever we were staying, but everything else was gone, including Dave's shoe, and other gear. So, we were stranded in Cardiff. We got ferried around by various folk people that day to do our various gigs, but the question remained of how we were going to get back home.

Fortunately, there was a chap called 'Barry the Bus', who

we knew vaguely. He had brought several people down to the festival from London and was heading back there, and he said he had enough room for me, Sam and the girls in his minibus. Dave would have to find some other way to get back. Wouldn't you know it, the blooming thing broke down on the motorway! I had to take my tights off to serve as an emergency fan belt, and the guys all peed into buckets to fill up the radiator!

And it doesn't end there! We all got home eventually, and it would all have been history, except that about a week later, we got a phone call from Barry the Bus. "You won't believe this," he said, "but I think I've just found your car."

"You're joking", we said. We had reported it to the police and posted notices everywhere, to no avail. But Barry was one of those guys who remembers registration numbers. He told us that it wasn't locked and that there were 24 cans of Carlsberg Special Brews in a case on the front seat.

"Right," we said, "we're coming now!" So we got ourselves to St Albans and Barry picked us up from the station and drove us to the car, which he'd left with somebody. Then we got in – fortunately we had a spare key, so we didn't have to jump-start it – and drove back to London, 24 Special Brews up on the deal. So there is some justice in the world!

Then there were the 'late night extras'. At folk festivals, there would be workshops and concerts going on all day. At the same time, usually in the local pubs, we'd have what we used to call 'sing-arounds', with everyone being offered an opportunity to do a 'turn' or music sessions with the occasional song where everyone jammed together. At some of them, around midnight, it would all end with a 'late night extra'. These were zany, crazy, anything-goes-type things, and they were always wonderful. After the ones at the week-long Sidmouth Festival, we'd move on to a pub called The Balfour, which had a big skittle alley at the back, where the landlord would do a 'lock-in'. If the police came round, we'd all have to fall silent, while he explained, "No, officer, there are no paying customers here, just a few of our friends." We'd sit up boozing for most of the night with people from all over the world, because Sidmouth was very international, ending up with a large breakfast on the sea front before retiring for a well-earned kip.

One night, I was with a lovely guy called John Maxwell, who was in a group that was gigging there. The following evening there was going to be something called the Bad Taste Ceilidh, with a prize for whoever came up with the most off-colour act. I was very well known for my bad taste in all things, so John and I decided we'd better write something for Sam and me to sing at the contest. We came up with what we called a Julie Andrews 'Mudley'. I can't remember all the lyrics, but it ended like this, to the tune of 'Supercalifragilisticexpialidocious':

[Dum di dum di dum di dum di] on the bed you're thumping
If you do it long enough it really feels like something,
Necrophilia, cunnilingus, [dum di] cocks and humping!

Well, needless to. say, when I came on stage and sang that with bright blue lipstick, red eyeshadow, and a rabbit stuffed into a belt around my tits, we won first prize!

As time went on, Mapesbury Road started turning into a bit of a folk music colony.

Lolly had moved out, as had David, who had gone to America shortly after Sam had moved into the bedsit vacated by the ballet people. David's departure may or may not have been a coincidence, in fact. Maybe there was a part of him that was in love with me, but he'd never been able to express it. Out of the blue, he asked me to come to New York with him. He'd got a job there and offered to take the girls and pay for everything.

I said, "It sounds like you are wanting to be in a relationship with me, but you aren't being clear."

"Well yes, I was hoping..." he said. At that point, I suddenly started to feel very angry, because it just seemed to be the Nick Goller situation all over again. You know, "You can come with me, but you'll have to share my bed." But I didn't say that. I was very close to David – even though he was introverted, I thought a lot of him, and he was really kind. For the record, I WAS tempted, but I had to make a decision, so I just told him I was in a new relationship and wasn't going anywhere. He went to New York on his own.

Anyway, Fanny was quite happy to let her spare rooms out to my folk music friends. First there was Sam, who took over Naomi and David's bedroom on the half landing. Then another folk act, Packie Byrne and Bonnie Shaljean, moved in. Bonnie rented Lolly's old room and Packie moved into Tanya's bedsit. Around this time, Sam and I started to be offered short folk tours, but how could we accept with my cleaning having to be done and the girls needing to be looked after? Two lovely friends came to the rescue, Elaine and Malcom. They were part of the set that ran the BBC Folk Club. Malcom was a high-up finance guy in the NHS, but Elaine didn't have a full-time job, so she offered to look after the girls to allow me to go on tours. They moved in while we were away and took Elayna and Mickie to school and so on. This made my life a lot easier, though I missed the girls terribly at first. Elaine wasn't able to have children of her own, which was very sad.

As part of the reshuffle at Mapesbury Road, things improved for me and the girls, accommodation-wise. Although life there was much more bearable than before, I still felt trapped and desperate to get out, so at one point I told Fanny I was planning to leave. She practically begged me to stay – she was getting on by now and didn't want change, plus she had started to see me as a daughter, or at least a daughter who cleaned. To persuade me not to go she said we could take on the now empty ballet studio on the top floor for minimum rent. It could become our living room, while I could move down to Sam's bedroom permanently. This would leave each of the girls with her own room, which they wanted very much by now. So that's what we did. I turned the old ballet studio into a wonderful living room/ dining room, and we had a decorating party to help get it ready.

Suddenly, we had space. The old ballet studio was very big, and we used to have great parties there. Our curry nights became legendary. We'd invite about 30 people and everyone would bring their own dishes, or mango chutney and poppadoms or whatever if they couldn't cook. We had four ovens between us all now, so we could keep everything warm. When we'd got everything ready, we'd go to the local Young's pub (which let the girls in too, though they shouldn't have), then come back to the house pissed as farts. We'd laugh, make music and eat curry for hours. It was just great!

There was a very funny incident involving Packie, who was quite elderly and an all-Irish whistle champion. One year, when we were all down at the Sidmouth Festival, his arthritis kicked in and he could hardly move, so he decided to go back to London. When he got to Mapesbury Road, he was in such a bad way that he just left his suitcase at the bottom of the stairs and crawled up to his bedroom on the middle floor. This was on a Friday. The following day, Fanny was having a Labour Party jumble sale at the house, and when she saw the suitcase, she just assumed its contents were donations for the sale. So she took all the dirty laundry inside it and hung it on pegs in the garden. This was just typical of her – she could be utterly clueless. Packie got quite a surprise when he came down the next morning and found all his filthy vests and pants on sale!

Fanny became very fond of my folk friends in her scatty way, and vice versa. But they could see what it was like for me working for her, and it was great for me having them around, as suddenly I had my own support group in the house. This was about to become handy for other reasons too, because in 1979, the year before we got married, Sam had a kind of nervous breakdown...

Sam and me in our music hall gear, around 1982

Taken at the Cardiff Folk Festival

'Semantics', a band we had in the '80s. Photo courtesy of Ian Anderson, Folk Roots

'Souvenirs of Sidmouth', a programme recorded by the BBC in the early '80s

8

FIVE YEAR PLAN

The Rising of the women, it makes me uneasy
The Rising of the women, it makes me unsure
Those strong freedom ladies tell me my life is wasted
Can't afford to believe them, can't help listening all the same.
— Chris Coe, *'Rising of the Women'*

I don't really know what caused Sam's mini-breakdown. His sister told me there might have been tensions in his relationship with his father, but I adored his dad and I think Sam did too. I have a feeling that a lot of his friends blamed me. They were mostly young people about town, with no responsibilities. When he and I got together, I think some of them resented the fact that he was no longer as free to do things with them as he had been before. Now he was with this woman with children and no money, it was harder for him to socialise freely. We couldn't just drop everything on the spur of the moment, and there were quite a lot of comments along the lines of "She's spoiling everything."

I can understand that I must have been difficult. I was always pushing and driving to get us out of poverty, so Sam must have felt under a lot of pressure, and maybe that's why his response was to cave in and become depressed. He quit his job on the Underground, and I'm afraid I wasn't very patient with him. I just thought, "What have you got to have a bloody breakdown about?" I told him that it was fine if he didn't want to get married, he could move out and do whatever he liked – free choice and all that. But no, he didn't want to do that. He really wanted to make a success of the music and practised for hours. My dreams of us being able to move out of Mapesbury Road and leave my cleaning life were dashed by the loss of his earning capacity. However, we were very much in love and determined to make a go of everything. Luckily, Sam's breakdown didn't last terribly long. We got married the following year (1980) in Brent, and had a wonderful day. Fanny held a reception for us, bless her, and the Cockerells all came to the wedding.

For a while, things were on the up. After a long gap, Sam had decided that he was ready to work again, so he got a part-time job in the civil service. Meanwhile, the music was going well and we were having a lot of fun with that. But as time went on, I became increasingly frustrated. I still felt trapped in Mapesbury Road and I was damned if I was still going to be a cleaner when I was 50. This was a really big thing for me, so as a first step, I got myself a part-time job as a lollipop lady!

I did it outside the primary school my girls had been to, although they'd now moved on to 'big' school. I'd always have sweets in my pockets, so the children would all come up to me. I was ever so popular! One day, I remember stopping a big dustcart to let the children cross the road and waving to them, saying, "Come on, come on!" But they wouldn't move.

"Oh no, miss, we'd much rather stay here watching you," they said. What a hoot!

That was good for my morale and earned me a bit of pocket money. It also gave me my first taste for many years of employment that didn't involve the Cockerell family. But it didn't last for long, because I had to have a hysterectomy at the age of 36. As I mentioned before, I'd always suffered from bad periods, and they'd started getting worse. During one performance, I had to come off stage because I was haemorrhaging so badly that there was a pool of blood. It was horrible. I'd seen Dr Naschen about the problem before, and he'd referred us to a consultant who was useless. I had five D&Cs to remove the lining of the womb but nothing showed up, so she accused me of having sexual problems! Then I got a second opinion from another consultant who examined me properly and told me that my womb was the size you'd expect three months into a pregnancy. It turned out the fibroids were on the outside of the womb. I had to have a hysterectomy to remove it, then I got an infection. I was very poorly for about six months.

During this time, the girls did some of the cleaning for me. I'd come down and do a bit whenever I could, which was usually for an hour or two each day, but the place was getting in more and more of a mess. This wasn't as much of a problem as it would have been before, since Fanny was getting doddery and didn't really notice. She'd even given up on those bloody candlesticks, although I'd still do them from time to time as a treat for her, because I was very fond of her by then. But I still made sure all the most important stuff got done.

I gradually started to get better physically, but I found myself struggling in other ways. I hadn't been fit enough to organise any singing work, and part of me felt that I didn't ever want to sing again. I didn't stick to that, but I did feel a desperate need to change my circumstances. I can remember vividly lying in bed while I was very poorly developing a Five Year Plan. There were three key elements:

1. Get fit again – this would start with learning to swim
2. Get a job that I could fit around my cleaning and musical commitments – this meant learning to type
3. Become independent of Sam – this meant learning to drive

These were all interrelated. I couldn't do anything without getting my health back, so I had to get fit again, and I had to be able to carry on doing the cleaning, at least for now, to keep a roof over our heads. But the most important thing from my point of view was being independent of Sam. When we had a row, he could storm off for a drive or go and see someone. I felt trapped. I wanted to storm out and leave him to look after the girls for once! To make that happen, I was going to have to learn to drive. But driving lessons cost money, and that was the main reason why I had to get a job that would fit round cleaning and the music.

I started looking around in the newspapers and shop windows and going for interviews, but the only place I could find that would be willing to work around my schedule was McDonald's. The nearest branch was in Kilburn. It was managed by a great guy called Billy, who had this fabulous blonde lady, Paula, as his deputy, and I started to do a bit of work there. It was horrendous at the beginning, because McDonald's was full of 16- and 17-year-olds and people who were moonlighting, which was still possible in those days. And they had a pyramid scheme, which meant that I, a well-spoken 36-year-old housewife, ended up being trained by people half my age. It was like the DHSS in Balham all those years earlier, only the other way around. They delighted in playing tricks on me and generally being quite nasty to me.

It was very, very hard going. I think I was paid £1.83 an hour at first, which wasn't a lot but at least it was something.

147

I remember having to clear up diarrhoea all the way up the two flights of stairs leading to the toilets! And the inside of the rubbish bins had to be cleaned with toothbrushes in the corners. Initially, I'd do my morning cleaning at Fanny's, walk down Kilburn High Road and do a shift from 1.30 to 5 p.m. Then I'd go home, except on the days when we had to leave London to perform elsewhere.

I made my way up through the ranks at McDonald's quite quickly because they sussed that I was good at things. Before long, I went on the till – I remember the singer/ actor Jimmy Nail coming in and being lovely to me. I started earning my 'white stars', which were awarded for quality, service, cleanliness and operational excellence, and they offered me more hours. I loved working and earning, so I took all the hours they would give me. If we weren't gigging, I would work from 1.30 p.m. till 11.30 p.m. They also decided that I should get involved with local marketing, which essentially meant doing the children's parties, where Ronald McDonald would appear and so on. By now, I was earning £3 an hour, which was a fortune in McDonald's terms. I was really good at those parties and the delighted parents would offer me tips. I always declined, but I'd say, "If you want to do something for me, could you write a letter to head office about me?" and hand them the address. Because what I was really after was a promotion that would take me off an hourly rate and give me a salary.

A lot of them must have actually done it, because Head Office became aware of what was going on at Kilburn with this strange woman, and sent people down to find out more. Then the guy who ran the whole of the UK and Europe at the time came to see for himself. I overheard him saying to Billy, "You only need one like that and you can double your income, you know." I was chuffed to bits! After that, I started doing all sort of marketing things, like getting involved with the local library, which was sponsored by McDonald's. I'd go in there and read stories, which would get children coming in who would never otherwise have gone to libraries. Then we'd get the local schools to send groups to the restaurant for readings. I also started up coffee meetings for elderly people, many of whom were lonely, and got them to introduce themselves to each other. We'd give them a discount and soon the place was packed, day in, day out. After a while, I was summoned to the head office in East Finchley to meet the head of marketing. I think she was called Jenny Walkinshaw, and she got me training other people to do the kind of thing I'd been doing in Kilburn.

Then I had a nasty setback. There was a flat above the store that was rented to a family on benefits, who were very anti-McDonald's. Our stockroom was on that level and one day, when I was heading up there, their teenage son set his big German shepherd on me. We reckon his intention was just to scare me and that he had timed it so I would open the door, hear the dog coming, then scarper. But being me,

I stopped to chat to his little sister, telling her what a great job she was doing sweeping the floor. This gave the German shepherd enough time to get to me and bite me. I had a huge bruise on my buttocks and had to be taken to hospital. The boy was taken to court, the dog was put down and it was all very unpleasant.

I was very upset and embarrassed and wouldn't go back to work at McDonald's for a couple of months. Then the new manager (Billy had left) came to see me at Mapesbury Road. He was another David and absolutely brilliant. "I hear you are still on sick pay," he said. "Are you planning to come back? I hope you are, because I've heard such great things about you." I agreed to start working there again and we became great pals.

After a while, McDonald's asked David and me to go as a team to open a new branch in Bethnal Green. He would be in charge of the property side of things, while I would be responsible for the human resources. I would have three weeks to recruit 112 people, get them on the pay roll, train them up and put them in uniform.

The regional director, who was a chap called James, told me that if I achieved all these goals, they would put me on a salary. This was the Holy Grail for me, because it would mean I could get rented accommodation. It was a fantastic opportunity, but obviously it had to be full-time. So I went to Fanny and begged her, saying "This is my big chance and I really, really, really want to do this. If I get the girls to do the

cleaning for you, will you give me these three weeks off?"
She was very frail by this time and she agreed. The girls
were pretty reluctant – they were about 16 and 14 by now,
so cleaning was far from their cup of tea – but they agreed
to do it, bless them.

By this time, I'd passed my driving test, at the third
time of asking, so that was one item ticked off my Five Year
Plan. I'd also learned to swim, as part of my fitness drive,
so that was another. This meant that I was able to drive to
the Bethnal Green job. But I kept getting lost. I remember
going round and round the roundabout at Old Street, not
knowing where I was, and in the end, just stopping the
car and bursting into tears. A huge line of vehicles built up
behind me, honking their horns. Eventually, a taxi driver
came up to me to find out what was going on. When he saw
the state I was in, he was an absolute star and led me to the
McDonald's.

If I say so myself, David and I were a brilliant team.
We worked really well together, and of course the Bethnal
Green job was invaluable training for my later career in FM.
I think David was impressed by my drive to succeed. We
probably worked 14 to 15 hours a day, and I was always
cheerful, even when I was very upset inside. It was an act,
but I was a performer, and my life had been a performance
for some time. I also had a knack of being able to get on
with people of all ages, backgrounds and ethnicities. I could
talk posh when I was with posh people and on the level of

the Eastenders when I was dealing with them. It just came naturally to me.

When the store opened, it had the third-highest takings for the first week in the whole of the UK. Obviously, McDonald's were delighted, so after I had gone back to doing my normal shifts at the Kilburn branch, I went to James the regional director and said, "Right, I've done everything you asked of me. When do I get my salary?"

"Oh, I'm sorry," he said, "I'm afraid that won't be happening because HR have blocked it. They say we'll have to go down a different route."

I was utterly devastated. David, who was now managing the new Bethnal Green store, came to see me one day and found me on my knees in the Kilburn stockroom, crying.

"This has really upset you, hasn't it?" he said.

"Yes, it has," I told him, "and I don't know what to do now."

"Anne, you could do anything," he said. I've never forgotten that. He had such belief in me, and he'd shown that at a time when I needed it more than ever. It was probably what kept me from having a complete breakdown over the next few weeks. They were bad enough as it was.

Looking back on it now, I realise that if it hadn't been for my time at McDonald's, I would never have got to where I am today. Yes, they let me down at the end, but it was a place where they gave people opportunities. They worked you damned hard, but if you did what was asked of you,

you got somewhere and you were on a ladder. That lesson stayed with me. But that's not how I saw it at the time. It felt like the end of the world. I had just been beginning to escape and suddenly the door had been closed on me. "I can't go through all this again," I thought.

I gave in my notice and left before the end of the week. Apparently, there was a huge hullabaloo about it at McDonald's afterwards, with people asking why on earth I'd gone, but I didn't find out about this until years later, when I bumped into someone who told me. What I do remember is the UK operations director calling me at home and asking me why I'd left, as I'd had such a bright future there. I don't know why I didn't just tell him that it was because James had welched on his promise. It must have been pride. Instead, I said that I had a new job now that paid me much more than I'd ever earned at McDonald's, and that I wouldn't go back there for anything.

Over the next few days, I came very, very close to falling apart. In fact, I'd say I had a mini-breakdown. I told Sam and the girls I didn't want to see them and shut myself in my room for a week, desperately trying to get my head together. But the one thing I did do was get them to bring me the Evening Standard every day, so I could look for a new job. We had a phone upstairs by now, so I was able to arrange interviews, and I got one with a firm that sold insurance for Irish Life. They offered me the job and I told Fanny that I wasn't going to clean ever again. During this period,

I remember aching with determination to finally get free of the cleaning and Mapesbury Road.

I was with the insurance company for about six months and I hated it. My job was to recruit young, intelligent people to work on a commission-only basis, and train them up and keep them motivated. The fact that they didn't get paid a salary offended me at my very deepest level, because I felt it was exploitation, and that went against all my left-wing principles. I also didn't like the CEO and founder at all. He was called Tony, and I thought he was a slimy git. But I felt I had to take the job and stick with it, because I didn't have the necessary experience – cleaning and McDonald's didn't really seem relevant – yet they'd taken a chance on me because they liked me. That seems to be how I have got a lot of my jobs over the years.

Anyhow, I'd only just started working at the insurance company when something momentous happened: Fanny died. It may even have been during my first week. I think it was pneumonia or a heart attack – we knew she was getting old, but I don't remember her being ill for a long time. To be honest though, I had been too preoccupied to pay much attention to whatever was going on with the Cockerells. I felt right on the brink of a major breakdown at this point, and when you are in that state you can only move forward. You are completely focused on the next 30 seconds and that's about it. I had no sense of what was going on in the rest of the world at all. I was very selfish and just obsessed with getting out of Mapesbury Road.

So it's bizarre, but I can't recall any of the specifics of Fanny's death. I definitely remember the funeral though. The family asked me to join them in the front row, which was lovely. I stood next to David, who had come back from America by this time. What wasn't so lovely was what Hugh said to me when we got back to the house. He took me to one side and said, "I don't want you working anymore. I want you to quit your job and go back to doing the cleaning, and I'm going to put the rent up for that room you've got on the top floor."

I know he must have been in deep grief and shock, but this was very hard to take after all I'd done for that family. I think people had been whispering to him about how ungrateful I was, which I felt was desperately unfair. When Lolly had had a baby, I'd been farmed out to help out for no pay – I was just told to go and do it. Something similar had happened when a friend of Fanny's had cancer. This time, I had been paid something, and the friend and her husband were lovely, but I'd resented Fanny thinking she could just hire me out without consulting me. It had felt a lot like slavery, and Hugh trying to force me back into my box was the final straw. It was typical of that family – everything was always liable to turn on a sixpence and you couldn't depend on anything.

"I'm sorry," I told him, "but that's it. I'm on strike now. I'm not going to do any more cleaning for you and I'm not going to pay more rent. You'll just have to evict us." Where I got the strength to do that, I have no idea, but I put my foot down. Not surprisingly, the atmosphere at Mapesbury Road was poisonous after that. Neither Hugh nor David, who had come back from America permanently and moved back in, would speak to me. It was dreadful – I'd bump into them on the stairs from time to time and they'd just blank me.

Obviously, the situation wasn't sustainable, so looking for somewhere else to live became a matter of urgency. I went to the council to see if I could get us housing, and it was like 1971 all over again. "You are leaving your current residence voluntarily," they said, "so we could put the girls into a B&B but we couldn't do anything for you and your husband." That was no good, so I went back to work at the insurance company determined to find a plan B.

I liked many of the people there, but because I found the job so troubling from a moral perspective, I kept looking for anything else that I could potentially do. After I'd been there for a month or so, I saw an advert in the Evening Standard for property managers for the London Borough of Haringey. There were three posts, one for each of Tottenham, Hornsey and Harringay (which is confusingly spelled differently when it refers to the area rather than the borough). The ad specified that women and people from ethnic minorities were particularly invited to apply. This was very early in the anti-discrimination days, but Haringey was a notoriously left-wing council, which of course appealed to my political side. So I thought, "What have I got to lose?" and sent off for an application form, which I filled in to the best of my ability.

To my amazement, I was invited for an interview. There were three people on the panel: Gordon, the head of property, a finance guy called Colin, and a lady called Jane Waterhouse, who I'm now friends with on Facebook. She told me afterwards that the only reason I'd got an interview was that I was the only woman or person from an ethnic minority who'd applied, and they had a policy that obliged them to interview a certain proportion of people from those categories, regardless of the standard of their application. They were not compelled to offer any of them the job, though. I didn't know that at the time of course, so I just went in and did my usual 'performance' thing.

I remember them saying, "Well you don't seem to have any relevant experience, so what would you do if, for instance, someone rang you up to say there was a leak at one of our properties?" I told them that by that time I would already have found out who the best people for mending leaks were and asked them in for a coffee, so I'd just ring them up and say, "I've got an emergency here, can you come and help?" They seemed pretty satisfied by this answer.

Then they asked, "What about budgets? You've got no budgetary experience."

"Oh no," I said. "I've been living on supplementary benefits for years. There's no difference. Just add a few noughts and it's exactly the same principle – you only spend what you've got, you put it in envelopes for when you need to pay the bills and you make sure that you don't run out of money."

They looked at me in amazement. Afterwards, apparently, they decided they liked me but couldn't justify giving me one of the posts because of my lack of experience. They had one in-house guy who was always going to get one of the positions, but aside from him, I was the only candidate who had impressed them. So they decided they had to re-advertise. I then got a letter from them saying that they didn't need to interview me a second time, but did I want to be considered for the second round? There was no guarantee that I would get the job, but they would keep me in mind if I wanted. So I wrote back and said, "Yes, please do that," but I never thought anything would come of it.

I decided that, although I had severe misgivings about my job with the insurance company, I'd better just get on with it until something else showed up. And I was good at it, almost despite myself. The system was that managers like me had six-person 'pods' working under them, and I recruited a fabulous young sales team. I also showed that I could be tough when I needed to be. There was one really cocky young man who thought he could do anything he liked. On his very first day, I put him on the phones, then he announced that he was going for lunch and didn't come back for two hours.

He swanned back into the office, took off his coat, and I turned to him and said, "You might as well put it back on." He asked me what I meant, and I told him he was fired.

"You can't do that!" he said.

"I most certainly can," I said. "Get your coat and go!"

He couldn't believe it. I had trouble believing it myself, because I wasn't a harsh person, but he'd deserved it. I felt quite proud of myself, and I think the other five youngsters in the pod were pleased, because they hadn't been taking liberties like that and it would have been death to the group if I'd let him get away with it. I recruited someone else and they were fine about it.

One of the good things about the company was that they laid on a lot of social events for the young salespeople and there were monthly prizes for the best performing pod. The people at the top created a good 'work hard, play hard' atmosphere. There were three of them: Tony, the slimy guy I mentioned before, and Steve and Tracey, who were very charismatic and good-looking. I got quite friendly with Steve and confided in him about why I had joined the company.

"Why were you so desperate to get a salary?" he asked me.

"Because I wanted to get out of Mapesbury Road, and if I had a salary. I could get a mortgage," I told him.

"Well," he said, "You are only earning £600 a month now – have you looked at whether or not that would get you any kind of mortgage?" I told him that I had done the figures,

159

but that it probably wouldn't be enough.

He then said, "I'm sure we can fake something. We're an insurance company, we sell mortgages as well as life insurance, so I'm sure we can sort something out. I'll talk to Tony for you."

So they faked papers to get me my first mortgage, overstating what my real salary was. I wasn't super-comfortable with this, as telling porkies wasn't my style, but as you know, I was in a desperate situation. By this stage, we were all in a state of panic – Elayna had moved into a squat and everything seemed to be falling apart around me – and sometimes you've just got to do whatever it takes. Plus, I was extremely confident that I would find a way of making the payments.

I was very grateful to the insurance firm, and also thankful to Steve for steering me away from buying one of the cheap council houses the Tories were in the process of selling off. We went to see one in Wandsworth, but he said, "Don't do it. The council will sell it to you cheap, but it will be in the middle of other council houses, the people who live in them will hate you and you'll never get your money back." I know that, in the long run, some of the people who bought council houses back then made a killing, but in the short to medium term it would have been a disaster.

In a way that you'll be beginning to recognise as typical of my story, at some point in this period I received a letter from Haringey Council offering me the property manager job in Hornsey. This meant that, in the end, we were able to buy a two-bedroom ground-floor flat in Hackney for £36,500. I got a mortgage with Halifax and the insurance company brokered the deal. For me, it was like the sun coming out. "I've done it," I thought. "We're on our way out of Mapesbury Road and now we're going to be property owners." I had achieved my Five Year Plan in more like two years and was absolutely elated. But for Sam and the girls, moving out of Mapesbury Road was a dreadful development. For them, life there had been ideal. They'd had their own rooms, lots of space and had been able to do whatever they wanted. Sam hadn't even had to work full time – I was the one who had carried the burden. I don't think I realised what a blow leaving there was for them all. Very quickly, our family unit would fall apart, but in the meantime I was over the moon at the prospect of finally moving out.

Actually, though, leaving the Cockerells' house was incredibly painful on an emotional level. As we were heading for the front door for the last time, I put my keys on the side and Hugh passed by me and blanked me completely. Then David came out of his room. I held out my arms to him and said, "Can't we have one hug before I go?" but he just turned around and went back into his room without saying a word. So that was the end of Mapesbury Road.

Years later, I went back to visit him there. We went up to the top-floor flat and he opened a cupboard. A cascade of sanitary towels that I must have forgotten to pack fell out of it. He clearly hadn't touched the place since I left and had kept it as a sort of shrine to our family. It was eerie, like the Mary Celeste.

I became a Ronald McDonald helper in the Kilburn branch in the early '80s

Children's reading sessions in the Kilburn branch of McDonald's, which I instigated with the local library.

The cleaning staff at Hornsey, Haringey

My second wedding, to Sam, 1980

9

BREAKDOWN

The beginning is now, and will always be,
You say you lost your chance and that fate brought you defeat
But that means nothing, you look so sad,
You've been listening to those who say you missed your chance.
There's another train, there always is
Maybe the next one is yours, get up and climb aboard another
train.

— Pete Morton, *'There's Another Train'*

nitially, I felt extremely optimistic after moving to Hackney. I had started the new job shortly after we'd moved and I thought, "This is it now! Elayna will come back from her squat, my marriage is going to survive and it's all going to be wonderful." But things didn't work out that way. First, Elayna refused to move out of her squat and into the flat. Then Mickie, who had come with us, started a sexual relationship with a guy called Clinton. which was illegal as she was only 15. Eventually, she ran off with him and left school, leaving me with no idea where she was for a while. In the meantime, things with Sam started to go seriously downhill.

As soon as we moved to Hackney, our rows started to get worse and worse. As I mentioned, he had a part-time job in the civil service by this stage, and he'd been having some counselling sessions with his boss, who he called 'The Colonel'. Somehow, Sam had convinced himself that I was not for him, that he'd never loved me and that I had manipulated him. I wonder even now if that was true.

I remember talking about all this with my great friend Julie McNamara, who is an award-winning dramatist/ singer/performer with mental health problems and the most wonderful person in the world. I told her that I needed to give Sam some space so he could sort himself out.

"He doesn't seem to know what he wants to do, and I don't know what to do with him," I said. She was just about to go abroad on a job for six weeks, so she asked me if I wanted to move into the squat she was living in, which was also in Hackney. She said it would be better to have someone there than to leave it empty, as this would prevent anyone else from taking it over. So I agreed to move temporarily out of our flat and into the squat.

As I was going out of the door with a few essential

possessions, I said to Sam, "Look, I don't have to go, we don't have to do this. All you've got to do is say that you love me, and we'll try again." But he told me he just couldn't say that. So I moved into Julie's squat, which was awful for me, as there was a pack of dogs living there who used to rifle through the bins up and down the staircases, and I was terrified of them after that incident with the German shepherd at McDonald's.

One day, Sam came round, sat on the futon, which was the main piece of furniture in the place, and said, "I've come to tell you that our marriage is over, that I don't love you and never have loved you." That was it, basically. Then he walked out and went back to our flat, while I was committed to staying in the squat indefinitely.

At this point, I decided that I could either throw myself in the canal or go to the local folk club and sing. You won't be surprised to hear that I went for the second option. I probably gave a particularly good and emotional performance, then I went back to the squat and heard nothing for days. "What the F is going on?" I thought. "He's living with *my* younger daughter in the flat that *I* am paying the mortgage for and doing nothing about anything." So, I rang his sister and his best friend and told them what he had told me: that we weren't ever getting back together. Meanwhile, he was still living in the flat, and I had to go back to it because I had a job that needed doing and my time at the squat was coming to an end. They were both very good about it actually. Sam agreed to move out and went to live with his sister. Later, he told me that he had been close to another breakdown at that point and hadn't known what he was doing or saying, but I was very, very bitter and hurt about it all.

Mickie had run off with Clinton by this stage, so when I moved back into the flat, I found myself living alone for the very first time in my life. It felt very, very weird. But by this time, I had begun having a wild affair with Ken, the borough engineer. I remember having mad sex with him up against a fence on Hampstead Heath in the summer of 1986, which shows what state my marriage was in by then. He was married too, so he was a very naughty boy, but I was a highly sexed person, and I hadn't slept with Sam for so long that part of me had moved on from him, and I let Ken woo me. I met his wife at one point. "You're not the first and you won't be the last," she told me.

Looking back on it now, I was walking on a tightrope for the entire period between my mini-breakdown in January 1986 and the proper one in September 1988. Being by myself just magnified the sense of instability. I threw myself into my work, like I'd always done, but I was very much in fight mode. I remember the chap who got the Tottenham property manager's job at the same time as I got the Hornsey one saying to me, "Anne, I don't know why you feel you have to fight everybody all the time. You are always fighting everything, and life doesn't have to be that way."

That made me step back a bit. "I'm pretty much where I

want to be," I thought, "so what on earth am I fighting? And why am I still doing it?" But that was the only way I knew how to operate back then. I had battles against my boss, and I got very involved with the unions, and it was always 'fight, fight, fight'.

On the personal level, the real problem with Sam and me breaking up was that most of our friends who lived in London were really his set. Just about all of them carried on seeing him but not many of them stuck with me, so my social life was drastically reduced. I'd still get invited to parties, but I wouldn't go because I couldn't bear to be in the same room as Sam. I did try to go to one party he was at, but I just ended up in floods of tears.

The break-up also affected my music life. The girls and I had been part of a Molly-dancing team – the only one in the country, in fact – called Paddington's Pandemonic Express, and I couldn't bring myself to continue with that because Sam was in the band, although the girls stayed on. But I carried on singing. I did quite a lot of solo floor spots and the occasional solo gig. And although the peripheral people in our circle had mostly sided with Sam after our break-up, my actual musician friends stayed incredibly loyal to me. Tom and Barbara, who had moved to London from Exeter, were particularly wonderful to me during this period. I'm also pleased to say that the girls and I reconciled very quickly.

I was still going to folk events and festivals, often with my dear friend Dave Hunt, who split up from his second wife around the same time as Sam and me. Lots of people wanted us to get together. I remember being at Sidmouth with him and everybody saying, "We'll get those two in a relationship and it'll be great." For me he was like a brother, so that was never going to happen! I did have other relationships though. I was definitely still seeing Ken, the engineer, in October 1987, because he was in my bed during the famous hurricane that month. I finished with him soon after that though, and started going out with a lovely guy called Chris Smith, who was a drummer, but a very bad one. He suffered terribly from anxiety and was six feet eight while I was five feet two, so we made a right pair.

By this time, I had formed a band with a couple of guys called Johnny Spires and Lee Collinson. Lee was very young but a brilliant guitarist. Johnny was a friend with a great voice who had been in a number of bands. He lives in Tenerife now, where he runs a disco. He was gay, but I remember going to a festival with him, sharing a tent and drinking lots of wine together. That got the tongues wagging!

It was while I was in the band with him and Lee that everything started to seriously unravel. We were performing at the Sidmouth Festival and were pretty good by then because we'd been playing together for about nine months. We packed out the Manor Pavilion, which was absolutely heaving before we even came on, and did the most magnificent set. Then I got a summer cold. I'd always had chest problems, but this one came down on me really suddenly. We still had to do this Radio 2 gig though. I got off on the wrong note, which was totally humiliating, as it was a live broadcast. I must have faffed my way through it somehow, but I remember being absolutely mortified. I felt really ill, and after that, I packed up the car and drove home.

I had a friend called June Tabor, who was and is well known in the folk world. I'd been singing jazz with her, which I'd learned to do in Leigh when I was 14 or 15 – I don't think I've mentioned this before, but I used to jam with a really good local jazz band there, who had been particularly impressed by my scat singing. Anyway, June was there at the festival with me, and later, when I was having my breakdown, she said, "You think it happened really suddenly, but it didn't, because during that week in Sidmouth you were crying nearly all the time." But I have no memory of that at all.

It was such a weird time for me, because I'd just started a new job at the Royal Postgraduate Medical School (RPMS) at Hammersmith Hospital. There will be more about that in the next chapter, but for now, the important thing to explain is that I was absolutely loving it. I was earning significantly more than I had at Haringey, I had a super, much bigger team and a wonderful, supportive boss, and I just knew I was going to be really good at the job. So this part of my life was a sheer joy. But then I'd come home in the evenings and do nothing but cry until it was time to go to work again. It was as if there were two completely separate, unconnected versions of me. One was thriving and the other was drowning. I didn't know what was happening but I knew I was in big trouble, so I cancelled going to the Towersey Folk Festival at the last minute. I felt terrible about this because I was letting Johnny and Lee down, just at the point when we were really starting to make it as a band. But I had no option. I was falling apart.

Then the 'car' dreams started. To give you a bit of background, I'd had a fabulous red car that I used to love driving, but I'd had an accident in it at some point during this period and sold it to my next-door neighbour for £100. I didn't realise I could keep it if it was an insurance write-off. Then tall Chris had got me an awful old clapped-out white car as a replacement. I had to drive it around the North Circular to get to the Hammersmith hospital, and I hated it because it felt so dangerous. The dreams started off as quick flashes, in which I would just be looking at the white car. Then they developed so I was now in it, feeling that this was all wrong and I had to get out. This happened every night and I'd wake up with a start every time. Then the dream evolved further – now I'd find myself in the white car at the top of a black spiral staircase that looked too narrow to go down. Next, the car started tipping into a vertical position, as if it was just about to head down the staircase. I didn't know when or how it was going to do this, but there was this oncoming sense of dread. By now, the dream was waking me up two or three times a night. Finally, on the night before I was due to do a gig at the Railway Club just outside Portsmouth, the car started falling down the staircase, but it never hit the bottom, because I'd wake up in terror before it got there. This happened every time I managed to fall asleep.

The weekend before the gig, I stayed at home working on stuff for the new job and fighting to keep myself together. On the Monday, I went into work as usual and remember very clearly having a meeting with the postal staff. I was completely compos mentis, talking to them about what I was going to do with the service and asking them how they felt about it. Then in the afternoon, which I'd taken off, I got on a train and went down to Portsmouth – obviously I didn't trust the white car to get me there. Originally, I had been booked to do the gig with Johnny and Lee, but they'd pulled out after me cancelling Towersey, so now I was due to do it on my own for this lovely guy called Sooty and his girlfriend Dee, who ran the club. So I took a taxi to Fratton, where they were living, and had a meal with them. Then, somehow, I got through the gig.

Afterwards, we sat around drinking and I told them everything that had been happening to me, including the car dreams. Dee, thank God, was a mental health nurse. When I'd finished talking, she took hold of my hand and said, "Listen to me Anne, you are in serious trouble. You can't go back to work and you need to see a doctor as soon as you get back to London." I told her I didn't have much faith in my doctor, so she suggested I should try to see someone at MIND.

We phoned up Ken, who I was still friends with, and asked him if he could find out how I could do that. After a while, he rang back and said he had arranged an emergency appointment for me with a chap called Nick at the Wembley branch of MIND. Then I called my boyfriend, Chris, who agreed to meet me at Waterloo. He drove me to where Nick was and waited outside while I talked to him. I went into a very small room and explained everything to him. He could see that I was imploding and that my situation was not sustainable. "You need to see a doctor. You can't go on like this and you need to be looked after," he said. "In fact," he added ominously, "we may already be too late."

He then rang my doctor and told him that I needed an immediate home visit. Chris drove me home to Hackney and, when the doctor came, he told me that he needed to send me to hospital. So we got back in the car and went to the Homerton.

I had the most awful experience in A&E. Chris had left me on my own there, because he didn't like hospitals, and this dreadful woman doctor kept saying to me, "What are you doing here? What's the matter with you?"

All I could say in reply was, "I don't know, I'll go home. I don't know, I'll go home." I was crying and crying and could hardly speak.

Eventually she said, "I'm going to have to get someone from our psychotherapy team down," as though this was a tremendous pain in the arse for her. Then somebody took me into a cubicle and talked to me for a while. I was terrified I would lose my job if I was off sick, so I probably tried to play things down, but they weren't convinced.

"We think you need to have a bed," they told me. "We need to bring you in, but we don't have any beds tonight, so we'll have to send you home. Is there anybody that can be with you overnight?"

"Potentially my daughters could be", I told them.

So they rang my daughters and said, "Your mother is seriously ill. She needs to be admitted to hospital, but we don't have a bed available. You need to be there with her tonight and take her to Hackney Hospital tomorrow, so that she can be admitted there." Chris came back to the hospital and drove me home, then the girls arrived – Elayna first and then Mickie. I think they were pretty upset. Elayna says I wasn't making much sense that night. The hospital had given me something to zonk me out, so I was probably talking gibberish.

The next morning, the girls took me to Hackney Hospital in a taxi. Elayna had called ahead to make sure they knew we were coming, but they turned out not to be ready for me. There were lots of people in the waiting room and I felt as though everyone was looking at me. I was so embarrassed, because here I was, this established businesswoman in a senior position with fancy nails and all the rest of it, about to be admitted into a psychiatric ward. I couldn't bear being looked at and flew into a blind panic, running into a corner of the room, hitting the wall, and batting away anyone who tried to come near me. Then I ran away and hid under a sink, or perhaps it was in a cupboard. When they found me, I was curled up in the foetal position. Then a doctor appeared, with his hands held up to show he wasn't going to hurt me. "It's OK," he said, "we've got you and you're safe now."

They took me over to Homerton Hospital and put me into an acute ward with both male and female patients. I had my own room, but there were people there who had been in and out of mental institutions all their life and I was terrified. It was an awful place to be. The guy who had admitted me took Elayna into a side room and I was in such a bad state that he gave her a sick note for me for an entire year. Fortunately, she had the presence of mind to telephone Nick, the man from MIND.

He knew how much I loved my new job and told her, "Do NOT let them issue that certificate, because if they do, your mother will lose her job. Go back and say to them that they must issue two-week certificates on an ongoing basis. Two weeks, then another two weeks, then another two and so on." Elayna was a real hero and persuaded them to do this.

She was only 18 or 19, and Mickie was two years younger, but they were left almost entirely on their own to look after me during this crisis. My friends, who I used to call 'the gang', should have been around to help the girls, but none of them came to their aid. Chris couldn't cope with the situation at all – he was just too traumatised. There was one friend, Su, who helped out and was very important at this time, but I find it very difficult to write about because much later we fell out over work and we are no longer speaking.

I was in that hospital for a month. They kept me so heavily drugged up that my memories of that time are mostly just snatches, but I do vividly recall nearly being raped one night. That was the worst moment of all, the real rock bottom. There was this tall, black patient trying to force his way into my room, and I was trying to keep him out by holding a chair under the door handle. I screamed and screamed but nobody came. Finally, the chair gave way and he came flying into the room, frothing at the mouth. Thankfully, at that moment the orderlies appeared and restrained him. When I saw him the next day, he was absolutely fine and had completely forgotten about it. But at the time, I had been absolutely terrified. I remember thinking, "Is this really what my life has become? Is that it now?"

I also remember my mother coming to visit me. She sat by my bed and I pretended to be asleep, because I couldn't face talking to her. Then there was this awful clinical meeting where they sat me in a chair in the middle of the room, with all the nurses, occupational therapists, psychotherapists and psychiatrists around me. By this time, I couldn't speak at all, so they just talked about me as though I wasn't there.

"Look at her nails, she's clearly been somebody with an important job in the past, but now look at her," and so on. I remember the utter humiliation of it all, the fact that I couldn't speak and had no voice. And they were talking about a person I didn't recognise – it wasn't me.

I wasn't sectioned, thank heavens, as that really would have been a problem for my future career, but I was completely at the mercy of whatever the doctors decided I could and couldn't do. After a while, they started to allow me to be taken out of the hospital for a walk during the day. My friend Su began taking me on brief visits to the flat, so I could sit in my home for a couple of hours. This was progress of a sort, but still, it was all just awful.

My daughters couldn't bear what was happening to me. Elayna, and I have her to thank for the rest of my life for doing this, decided to ring Nick at MIND to ask for his advice.

"They've got her on drugs all the time and she's not getting any better," she told him. "We just don't know what to do. They don't seem to be giving her anything that is helpful." Nick advised her to ring Neil Gershon, my fabulous boss at RPMS, to ask whether there was anything Hammersmith Hospital could do to help.

"All we can do," Neil said, "is refer her to Occupational Health. You will have to get her here in a taxi and then we'll see what they say."

So that's what happened. My girls took me out of the Homerton and back to the flat, and because they had been told I couldn't be left on my own, for the next few weeks they either both stayed with me there or took it in turns. Then Elayna took me to Hammersmith Hospital to see the occupational therapist, who was a lovely guy. By this time, I had regained my voice. For quite a while when I was in the Homerton, Su had told me, it had been like the voice of a three-year-old. She had found that very scary. In fact, a lot of people who knew me had been frightened by what happened to me, because they thought, "If it can happen to Anne, it could happen to any of us."

The occupational therapist spent an hour talking to me and at the end he said, "You know what? You are very in touch with yourself, which is an extremely positive sign." Then he asked Elayna to come in. "I'll have to speak to the Head of the Department and we'll need to get your mother assessed," he told her, "But if we refer her to the psychiatry department, she will probably need to come in once a week. Would you be able to bring her in for her appointments?" Elayna, bless her, said that she would. I don't know how she managed to get the time off work, but once a week, she would come to the flat, put me in a taxi and take me to the Hammersmith Hospital, until I was well enough to go by myself.

The psychotherapist I saw there, David Zigmond, is one of the most inspirational, wonderful people in the world.

He said that there was a healthy inevitability about my breakdown and that it had been brewing for years. He also said there had been a kind of pendulum effect. At long last, I'd got myself into a position when I was safe and relaxed, then everything had just hit me and sent me flying in the opposite direction. But that had needed to happen. It was the two previously disconnected sides of me coming together – the hyper-efficient workaholic and the broken trauma survivor, and it had taken a major meltdown to bring that about.

He was totally on my side about everything. I told him about stealing Fanny's money and he said, "Look what she stole from you." And all the sexual abuse stuff came out, of course. In fact, I started to talk to other people about it, including my mother, who asked my sister whether she believed it. She said she did and had always been wary of my grandfather too. Dr Zigmond told me I had done very, very well to survive it and still be a human being. He was simply marvellous with me, and really wanted to see me back at work.

Slowly, I started to improve. They took me off some of the zombie-like medication and Dr Zigmond found the right drugs to begin stabilising me, so by November time, though I was still very, very shaky, I was becoming me again. I vividly remember pulling up the lovely, old fashioned sash window in my bedroom one cold, sunny day, and planting some bulbs in the window box. It was a sign that I was starting to believe I would be around in the spring to see them flower. It felt like a very important and powerful thing to do for myself, because it was a symbol of hope.

After Christmas, Dave Hunt, the lovely guy who everyone had wanted me to get off with at Sidmouth, came to stay for a weekend. He took me to the folk club I'd been going to before everything went pear-shaped. It was the first time I had really been out of the flat apart from those taxi rides to my therapy appointments, so I was very nervous. I didn't actually go into the club – I just sat near the entrance, not saying much to anyone – but it was a big step forward.

I was still off work when the bulbs I had planted bloomed, but those flowers felt like a tangible sign of my recovery. I could remember how frail I had been when I'd planted them and contrast that with how much better I was feeling now. Not long after that, the hospital started gradually phasing me back into my job, initially on a very part-time basis. I had been off work for seven months in total, six of them on full salary sick pay, so had been really lucky in that sense. I continued having appointments with David Zigmond for two years.

Neil Gershon was an absolute star throughout my illness and beyond. I'd only been in the job for six weeks when I'd had my breakdown, so I'd had no rights at all, but he'd fought for me because he believed in me. He'd been under a lot of pressure to get rid of me, as the woman who'd had my job before me had been unable to hack it and had left after a few months. "Here we go again, another flaky woman," his bosses had said. "You'll have to fire her." But he had resisted, and I'll be eternally grateful to him for that.

A few years after I'd left RPMS, I invited Neil to my 50th birthday party. He wrote Elayna a wonderful letter to explain why he had given me the job and what he thought of me:

It is difficult to distil my memory of Anne to a few sentences. I suppose the first impression lasted the longest and the second was the most important.

Anne came for interview for the post of Premises Manager at RPMS on the strength of a somewhat thin CV. I thought it was a bit chancy given her experience but the vibrancy of the application made me think I should meet her. Anyway, we ended up talking for about one and a half hours – I say 'we' but in fact Anne talked for about 85 minutes and I think I got the odd word in. Most of the time she talked about her hysterectomy and how it had changed her life etc. For some reason I still do not understand, I gave Anne the job. I think she was the first person who could shut me up and I felt absolutely sure that she would do a root and branch job on the maintenance and premises staff in the School. The end product was so successful that I credited myself with incredible intuition and insight. Probably the most successful appointment I have ever made.

My second recollection is of a frightened and confused person who had suffered a nervous breakdown and who was desperately keen to fight it and get on with the job she had just won. I developed an enormous admiration for Anne's courage in fighting her illness and was so incredibly pleased that she came through it to make the real contribution to RPMS that I knew she was capable of. From a selfish point of view I was thrilled that my faith in her had been vindicated. From a human standpoint there was no-one more delighted than me when Anne came back to work and made a full and lasting recovery.

Anne is a very special person with tremendous courage and a great deal of ability. Believe me there aren't many like her.

In 2013, when I received my award from the British Institute of Facilities Management for the profound impact I'd had on the industry, I made sure Neil Gershon and Dr Zigmond were there at my table, because I owed everything to them. Or rather to them and my daughters, who had stood by me during that awful period, which was what had made life worth living and fighting for again.

That breakdown was the real turning point in my story. Everything up to that point was leading up to it, and since then, things have been different. There have been tough times, for sure, but never on that scale, and instead of feeling like I am going around in circles, my subsequent life has mostly been a case of 'onwards and upwards'.

As I became better and stronger, I became increasingly convinced that the breakdown was the best thing that had ever happened to me. I could feel myself changing. I didn't have to fight anymore and could finally let go. The pressure had gone. I continued to be a hard worker, but I didn't constantly have to prove myself anymore, and I was no longer perpetually at war with everyone and everything.

So, a big part of why I'm telling my story is to say, "It's OK to have mental health problems." I have made several speeches on the subject, even when it wasn't fashionable to get up and admit you'd had difficulties. Things are improving, but there's still a stigma attached. I want to stand up and say, "There's no need to feel ashamed, you know." Because although, at my worst, I was completely dysfunctional and couldn't even speak at one point, I was never ashamed, and maybe that's how I got through it all. If my story can inspire other people in crisis to do the same, writing this book will have served its purpose.

I also want to say to employers, "If you've got somebody suffering from something like I went through, they are not going to get over it quickly, but they can do it with the right support. They may even be better workers afterwards than they were before, and I'm the living proof."

In the Dove at Sidmouth with June Tabor, about a month before my breakdown

On stage with Johnny and Lee at Sidmouth a month before the breakdown.

With daughter Elayna shortly before my breakdown – no signs!

Me about seven months after my breakdown

10

WHY FM IS SEXY

What Is It You Do?
It's a role that requires superhuman abilities,
awesome the range of the responsibilities.
Tell them your job they don't know what the hell it is.
That's what you find when you manage facilities

Workplace or care home or top university
benefits from optimised capability.
Wellness, efficiency, sustainability,
that's what we bring to a well-run facility

Buildings that work through a maintenance system
that helps your firm cut its costs and its risks, then
finding your desks much more clean than you left them.
That's what you get when you hire an FM

Healthy, secure, the prevention of accidents,
there for your most unpredictable incidents,

expert responders with skill and with common sense.
That's what we do in facilities management.

– Martin Pickard

I haven't said much about the Haringey job until now because there was so much else going on around then that it would have felt disjointed to go into detail about it alongside descriptions of my marriage break-up and nervous breakdown. But it becomes relevant now, because it was my first proper taste of FM, and from here on in, that's what much of my story is about.

Not that my role was described as facilities management back then. I was area property manager for the Hornsey section, and I absolutely loved it. I was in charge of the town hall, which is a wonderful Art Deco building, plus the theatre and boxing rings next to it. I also had nine other office buildings in the Hornsey area to look after, including the housing building and the one where the architects were. Then there was a converted church up in Muswell Hill, which had its roof blown off by the great storm of October 1987 – that kept me busy. But what, you may well be wondering, did the job actually entail?

People are always asking me what facilities management is. I think my pal Martin Pickard has answered the question perfectly in the poem above, but I'll also give you my own definition. For me, FM is everything that supports people doing their work, particularly their working environments and the infrastructures that surround them. Take me working from home, for example. The role of FM would include doing a risk assessment to make sure that I wasn't going to damage my back. I'd be looking at my chair and the way the space was organised, to make sure that I wasn't twisting it in a potentially harmful way.

On the other hand, making sure my computer was hooked up to the network so I could participate in Zoom meetings would probably be a job for IT. One of the trickiest things for people outside the business world to get their heads around is the division between FM and IT departments, not least because the two tend to work very closely together. Part of the problem is that, when the term 'facilities management' first came to the UK from the US where it originated, it was hijacked by two different kinds of organisation: premises or property management, which was what I did, and IT. I remember going to what was billed as an FM conference which turned out to be just about IT. It was very confusing and it took about five or six years in the 1980s for the terminology to settle down.

In the end, it was generally agreed that facilities management was about the physical environment, IT about the virtual sphere, and human resources about the people. I always worked very closely with my HR colleagues because, as you will see, my approach to FM has always been very people-focused. Increasingly, FM, IT and even HR are getting lumped together under the umbrella term 'workplace'. This reflects the fact that the support functions within an organisation often overlap. And workplace itself has been changed forever by the Covid pandemic. Now the new technologies enable people to work from almost anywhere as long as they have stable connectivity and the right tools.

Anyway, rather than spending all day trying to give a watertight definition of FM, I'll try to convey to you what it's all about as we go along. A big part of the answer is establishing and supporting what we call BAU, or 'business as usual' (there are lots of acronyms in facilities management!). Say you go into an office building. You start off at reception, which is run by FM, then you either show your ID card, or if you are a visitor, you go through some kind of signing-in process (customer experience is a big part of facilities management). Either way, it falls under the remit of FM. Then you get into the lift, which is maintained by FM, and walk to an office, where everything from the chairs and desks to the air-conditioning is sourced and looked after by FM. The telephones may be too, although that side of things increasingly falls to IT. It didn't when I first started out, though. At Hornsey, I was in charge of an old-fashioned switchboard, with a team of eight girls and a supervisor.

Sometimes, though, FM is the polar opposite of BAU. A case in point is the toilet incident at the Hornsey town hall, which is one of the best stories from my time with Haringey Council, provided you haven't just eaten. It was the Friday before a bank holiday weekend and there was a blockage under the building, so the whole place had flooded and the lift was eight feet deep in turds. I got the Dyno-Rod-type people in and they asked to see the drawings of the plumbing system. Ken the engineer and I tried to look for them, but unfortunately, they had been lost over the years, so they just had to guestimate where to insert their jetting nozzle to clear the drains. The water and all the rest of it whooshed out where Ken had predicted it would, leaving one hell of a mess – I had to get the disaster recovery people in to pump it all out and put straw down – but the problem seemed to have been sorted. What we didn't find out until an hour later was that a magician had been sitting on the toilet in the theatre next door at precisely the moment when the plumbers had jet-blasted the system. One minute he had been quietly reading his paper, the next he had been shot upwards by a violent torrent of God-knows-what. I think he may have hit his head on the ceiling!

So that's the kind of thing you find yourself dealing with when you're a facilities manager. You have to be prepared to deal with just about anything. It is never boring and that is what makes it such a great career.

A big part of what I had to deal with at Haringey was

politics. One major issue was compulsory competitive tendering (CCT). This was a Conservative government initiative which meant that local authorities were forced to open up in-house services like refuse collection to private competition. The idea was to reduce costs and increase value for money, but of course the unions resisted it like anything. Meanwhile, the councils were obliged to go for the cheapest options, which incentivised organisations to come up with artificially low bids, in the hope that they could up their prices once they got the work. But often they couldn't, which meant that the whole thing was disastrous: standards went down, relationships fell apart and it was a disastrous beginning to what has now become quite a sophisticated outsourcing environment, although the unions still don't like it.

Haringey was a very left-wing local authority. Obviously, some of what went on there was in tune with my political beliefs, but it was a crazy time. At one point, a lot of people were vociferously protesting against the council using black rubbish bags, on the grounds that they were racially discriminatory. I got a quote for red ones, and when they found out how much that was going to cost, the idea was quickly dropped.

There were also lots of women on the council who wore dungarees and little pince-nez glasses and spent their whole time slagging off men. I didn't have any problem with men – in fact, I got on famously with them. This meant I got much more done than the women in question, so they hated me. But I was a feminist too and did a lot of good work on behalf of women. I had a big workforce of cleaners, all of whom were female. The problem was that their trade union rep was a man, and he was much more interested in looking after the male workers, like the porters and the security staff, than the women. So, I took up their cause in a big way, particularly in regard to the AIDS crisis. What was happening was that women cleaners were going into public toilets to clean them with absolutely nothing in the way of protection against the needles drug users left behind or all the bodily fluids that needed clearing up. This was a time when everyone was completely terrified of AIDS, but at the beginning, nobody was doing anything to safeguard these women.

Unlike most people on the council, who couldn't have cared less about health and safety (H&S), I found it absolutely fascinating. This was because it was all about people – keeping them safe and getting them to think about other people's safety as well as their own. As you can imagine, after living in Fanny's ridiculously dangerous house for 15 years, this was something of a passion of mine. Anyway, nobody else in the property department wanted to be part of the Haringey H&S Committee, so I put my hand up and said that I would do it.

As time went on, I started to make a bit of a name for myself on that committee, but at the first meeting I went to,

I thought that I'd better keep very quiet as I knew nothing about H&S apart from what I had come across while working at McDonald's. There were 40 men in that room, plus me, and most of them were waffling on talking absolute bollocks about the AIDS situation. There was no protocol for the women cleaning the public toilets, no protective kits or anything. They weren't actually my workforce – this was streets and cleansing and I was just responsible for the insides of office buildings – but I felt that I had to make a stand. So, I started doing a lot of research, calling up people in America and asking them what they were doing about street toilets over there and so on. Then, at my third meeting, I decided I was going to speak out.

I was absolutely terrified, so I decided to go in there with no knickers on. This may not seem like the most obvious solution to you, but I thought, "I'll know and they won't," and somehow it gave me confidence. It enabled me to say to them all in my head, "You pompous men think you know everything about everything, but actually, you don't even know that I'm not wearing any underwear." I thought it up on the spur of the moment. I was so scared I didn't know what to do, then I just thought, "Right, pull yourself together, woman," went into the loo and whipped off my knickers. Then I put them in a pocket and walked into the meeting room. Part of the infamous 'imposter syndrome', I suppose.

Despite my fears, when I said my piece, they did actually

listen to me. New research had been coming in that showed that, in Africa, women and children were catching HIV, so it wasn't just a problem for homosexual men and intravenous drug injectors. This, of course, had upped the fear level, but they had been debating the subject in a very 'high', abstract way, and I brought it right down to earth.

"Look," I said, "we have got some of our people who are in danger of catching it NOW. We need to think of practical steps we can take to protect them, what we need to get and how we are going to do it."

I became part of the group that was set up to deal with the issue. First, we established the policy, which is what always happens in the public sector. Then we started issuing the cleaners with personal protective equipment (PPE), which everyone is familiar with now because of Covid-19 but they weren't back then. We gave every team one of those yellow sharps boxes that they have in hospitals, and a process they had to follow when they were dealing with used needles. We also gave them a special gel to put on top of vomit or blood if they came across it, which rendered it safe to shovel. Then everything had to be triple-bagged into clinical waste sacks. Developing the policy was incredibly interesting and rewarding for me.

I haven't said much about working at Hammersmith Hospital either, because my job there had only just started when it was rudely interrupted by that almighty nervous breakdown. But now is the time to pick up the story.

The Hornsey job had been great, but after a couple of years there, I felt ready for a new challenge. I wanted to take the next step up the FM ladder and was looking for something better paid. I also, frankly, wasn't getting on terribly well with Gordon, the head of property for the borough. So, when I saw an advertisement for the post of premises manager at the Royal Postgraduate Medical School at Hammersmith Hospital, it felt like a no-brainer. I only got my application in at the last minute, though. I wrote it by hand, with the help of several of the Haringey engineers, then I delivered it in person to meet the deadline

Neil Gershon explained, in that letter in the last chapter, why he felt compelled to give me the job, despite my limited credentials. Although everything went to pieces almost as soon as I started at RPMS, I knew as soon as I got there that I had absolutely arrived. Haringey had been good, but this was in another league entirely. To give you an example, Hammersmith Hospital gave me my first laptop, which was a Toshiba that cost £4,000. That would be expensive now, never mind then. I also got involved in much bigger projects than I had at Hornsey. At one point, I was the client for a new £16 million clinical research building they were putting up, leading a team of architects, structural engineers, mechanical and electrical consultants – the works. I was responsible for everything from the bogs and the boilers to the design of the overall environment and keeping it safe. I found it all unbelievably fascinating.

I was therefore terrifically motivated to get my act together when I went back to work after my breakdown. I also needed to get earning again. After six months off on full salary, my sickness pay had reduced to half, but Neil, bless him, organised a staggered return for me. This meant that they paid me extra for every bit of work I did, which further incentivised me to get going again.

The first thing Neil asked me to do when I went back to work was a review of the cleaning system. I'd be lying if I said I hit the ground running. For the first few weeks, I hid myself in the office. I couldn't answer the phone or talk to people: I just concentrated on writing the specification for the cleaning project. Neil was fabulous – he would come down when I was working late and tell me, "You are doing fine. It will all be alright, just keep going."

The cleaning system I had inherited in the RPMS, which was the area I was responsible for (I managed about 18 buildings out of a total of 65), was appalling. The whole place was filthy. One of the first things I did, which I still do now as a consultant when I've got anything to do with cleaning, was go around inspecting the equipment cupboards. In a well-run institution, the vacuums will have their portable appliance testing certificates on them, there will be a COSHH (control of substances hazardous to health) risk assessment sheet on the wall, and everything will look clean and well-organised. What I found in the first cupboard I looked in at RPMS was a bottle of Fairy Liquid and a load of mops standing in buckets of dirty water. The vacuum, which was encrusted with dust, had just been left in the corridor. All the other cupboards I looked at were equally horrendous. "I can't fail to improve on this," I thought.

With the help of David Field, who was a lovely guy who worked in the main hospital, I developed what is known as an 'output specification' for the cleaning at RPMS. I then ran a procurement exercise with six cleaning companies to see which one I could get the best deal from, with expert advice from an external consultant called Steve, who was Dave's mate. The company that I liked best at the interview stage was actually the one that came up with the cheapest bid. But I knew, from my experience at Haringey, that they were never going to be able to give me the standards that I wanted for the price they had quoted. It was the usual pattern – as with compulsory competitive tendering, they had come up with an implausibly low quote to make sure they got the contract.

Still, I wanted them to do the job, so I came up with an original solution. "I am going to give you a one-off lump sum," I said. I have a feeling it was £5,000 but it might have been £12,000. "And I want you to use it to clean certain areas of the school up to a high standard. Then after that, I want you to carry on doing the cleaning at the rate you tendered – which shouldn't be too difficult because you'll be starting from a point where everything is as it should be."

The company, Pall Mall, couldn't believe it. Nobody had

ever offered them more money than they had bid for before, so they practically bit my hand off. But on the very first day of the contract we had agreed with them, none of the cleaners they had recruited showed up. I got on the phone to their managing director and said, "I want you down here NOW with your directors, and I want you to clean, because I am not going down for this after everything I have done to support you." And do you know what they did? The managing director, the sales director and the operations director came down to RPMS, rallied the cleaners who hadn't shown up, pulled in some extra ones from other sites, and while they were waiting for them to arrive, they got down on their hands and knees and started cleaning. They stayed there all day, in fact. It was the beginning of a very good working relationship, because I had shown them I was willing to stick up for them, but only if they did their part.

I got a lot of mileage out of my willingness to fight on behalf of the people who were working for me. One day during the six weeks I had at Hammersmith Hospital before my breakdown, my maintenance supervisor, Steve, came into my office with a horrible burn on his arm. I remember it well because it was a lovely sunny day, he was in shorts and a sleeveless T-shirt, and he was damned good looking! I asked him what on earth he had been doing to get that burn.

"Been doing a confined space, ain't I?" he said. "The

Ogden pump needed a bit of this and that doing to it and the hospital needs its hot water."

I then asked if anybody had been with him and he said they hadn't. "I want to see to see where this is," I told him. He led me to this manhole, which led into a space a person could only just get into, filled with hot water pipes. He'd gone down there with no oxygen mask, no PPE and nobody at the top to make sure he was OK. I was horrified.

I brought him back to the office, sat him down and said, "Right, I am going to give you a formal warning." He looked at me as if I was absolutely mad. "You will NEVER do this again," I told him. "You will always make sure that you take care of yourself, you wear the appropriate clothing and make sure you've got somebody with you. Do you think for one minute that if there had been an escape of hot water or gas and it had got to your eyes that the organisers of this hospital would have looked after you for the rest of your life? No, they wouldn't. They'd pay you off and you'd be gone, sitting there blind for the rest of your life. Do you really want that?"

Steve had only been trying to do what he thought was the right thing – he was absolutely dedicated to keeping the hospital going. But he got my point and never did it again. Coincidentally or not, when I went back to work after my breakdown, we started having a relationship. This was really good for my confidence. It also meant that he had my back, which came in very handy as I started getting into all kinds of conflicts with Tony, the guy who had been my deputy before my breakdown and now was in charge of projects, together with a new guy called Nigel, who Neil had had to bring in during my long absence.

Initially, I had been brought in to run both the premises and projects, and I would have done a blinding job if I hadn't become ill. But by the time I went back to work, they had been split into two separate departments, with me as the premises manager and Tony the projects manager. We both reported into Nigel, who struck me as one of those people who loved to swan about pontificating but never got his hands dirty. I wanted to run things properly but he and his sidekick Tony, not so much. I felt they tried to undermine me at every step.

Not long after I went back to work, there was a project for one of the laboratories that Tony had been supposed to be running, but he hadn't put anything in place to get it done. He had given the client a date, but he hadn't booked the work in with the contractor and there was no risk assessment or method statement. So I went to see the professor who ran the lab, and he absolutely tore me to shreds. All the projects had run perfectly until I came back, he told me. Tony was fine and I should keep my nose out if it. As you can imagine, this kind of thing created huge tension between the projects department and my department. Eventually, the professor and I got on famously and he apologised to me for his outburst that day.

It took time to gain trust after my breakdown.

Then there was the fire alarm fiasco. There had been a long history of things going wrong with the system, and Nigel and co had come up with a plan for a new central fire alarm panel that Steve the maintenance supervisor and I just knew wasn't going to work. This was potentially a matter of life or death, so we went over Nigel's head to Neil and told him we would both resign if he insisted on going ahead with installing this dodgy system. Neil listened carefully and agreed to change the plan and have us run it – but he warned us that if anything went wrong, it would be serious for both Steve and myself. Actually, I had great fun doing all the risk assessments, and getting teams of extra security people in to patrol all 13 floors of the building in the gap between them ripping out the old alarm panel and installing the new one. We eventually got everything sorted, but at first the alarms kept going off for no reason, and I was perpetually having to deal with the teams of three fire engines that would then arrive. They were obliged to send out that many because we were a hospital.

Mind you, flirting with handsome firemen in yellow suits was fun too!

The three Area Property Managers at Haringey. I learnt so much from these guys

My very first business publicity shot, taken in 1992

Members of my staff at RPMS Hammersmith Hospital. Still my favourite job ever

11

ANNE LENNOX-MARTIN MSC

So come on all you women if you feel you're missing out
The right to lead your own life is worth finding out about
Nothing without struggle
Always a price to pay
Exploring's always risky,
Don't let that stand in your way!

— Anne Lennox-Martin, *Self-Made Woman*

I did a lot of innovative things at RPMS, like creating the 'One Team'. This involved amalgamating all the different support services I was in charge of – my porter staff, security contract, administrative people, reception and maintenance – into one big, co-ordinated team. The idea of a One Team was a fairly new concept, and I didn't know anyone who was doing it in the public sector, so it was pretty revolutionary. I also introduced an electronic help desk system with each job having a unique number. Computer-aided facility management (CAFM) systems were in their infancy, so this was pretty groundbreaking for the time.

I became quite well-known for talking about these things at seminars and conferences.

Those kind of events really suited me, because I was never intimidated by being in a so-called 'man's world'. I remember being at a seminar about the 'Six Pack' legislation on pressure vessels, which was a raft of new health and safety regulations introduced at the start of 1992. There were 200 men there and just two women – me and the tea lady – and I had a great time. I just refused to accept that it was a problem. In fact, not being male worked to my advantage. I stood out, so all the men would be dying to ask me, "What are you doing here and how did you get into all this?" I was a born-again flirt, so it was a bit of a case of bees around a honey pot. And of course, being men, they would love explaining things to me. I wasn't too proud to say, "I haven't come across that before, please tell me about it," so I'd pick up all sorts of useful information. I'd giggle my way through everything, bat my eyelashes and come away having made some really good contacts or learned something important. I know my women colleagues will be a bit horrified to hear this, but in those days I had no other way of gathering all the knowledge I needed. I was also genuinely fascinated in how mechanical and electrical systems worked, as well as the new access control and building management systems, which were only just coming in at that time.

It was through the seminar/conference circuit that I got to meet John Jack, who is an important figure in the next part of my story. By this time, I'd started doing a master's degree in facilities and environmental management, sponsored by Neil and the RPMS. I'd read an article in a magazine called *Premises Management* about an architect called Professor Bev Nutt, who was planning to set up the first English MSc in the subject at University College London. "Aha," I thought to myself. "Here's a chance for me to get a proper qualification." I was able to get in touch with Bev through Richard Byatt, the journalist who had written the piece, and I took him out to lunch.

"Right, when are you going to start this course?" I asked him. "Because I want to be the first on it." Bev told me that he hadn't even started planning it yet, so I said, "Well, come on then, get on with it!"

Bev teamed up with a guy called David Kincaid, who had been IBM's London regional property manager, and together they devised this fascinating course. It was an architectural qualification, run by the Bartlett School of Architecture, and what was so innovative about it was that it brought together architects and FM people. Previously, there had been huge arguments between the two professions, because architects wanted to build buildings which looked lovely and won them prizes, while facilities managers wanted buildings that were fit for purpose and wouldn't cost a lot of money to run. Architects thought FMs were low down in the pecking order, and FMs saw architects as arrogant twats. The genius of what Bev and David did was to bring the best of architecture and the best of FM together to create a qualification that enabled FM people to speak the language of surveyors, structural engineers, architects and so on, and vice-versa. It made FM a proper profession, not just a matter of bogs and boilers.

There were seven of us who went on the original course in 1992, so of course we called ourselves The Magnificent Seven. We were a bit of a motley crew. There were two women – me and a lady called Jackie, who was a project manager but wanted to get into FM – and five men. They included a lovely guy called John, who was a maintenance person, and a semi-retired chap called Ken, who was writing a book about facilities management but had never actually done it. UCL recruited fantastic lecturers for us, many of whom were very famous within the industry, like Oliver Jones, who was one of the pioneers of FM.

I had to have day release to do the MSc, but Neil Gershon was marvellous about that, and RPMS said they'd pay for it provided I could do my week's work there in four days. I couldn't, of course – I had to do lots of work at home. But I managed to get on the course, which was quite an achievement given that my only qualifications were two A-levels with distinction. They set a special exam, which gave me the opportunity to prove that I knew what I was talking about. The whole thing was a huge boost to my confidence, at a time when I had very little of it. People who remember me from that time might not realise that, because I was very outlandish and outspoken at events, but I was still getting over the breakdown, and the MSc helped a lot.

Anyway, to get back to John Jack, he was a former property director at IBM who had got together with about 90 of his colleagues to buy out the company's FM division. They had then built it up into Procord, the world's very first 'total outsourcing FM company'. John, who had been the visionary behind the project, was now its managing director. We often used to find ourselves speaking in back-to-back slots at conferences and seminars, because he represented one side of the coin – outsourcing – while I represented the other one, namely building and managing in-house teams. But the striking thing was that we were saying exactly the same thing: if you treat people well and motivate them, they will do a good job. Ultimately, it didn't matter all that much whether they were in-house or outsourced. The important thing was to make the people on the front line feel genuinely valued, and to get them to know each other so they would help each other out.

John and I often used to talk to each other during coffee breaks and so on. One day, after we had been speaking at a conference in York, we were due to catch the same train back to London. We got chatting on the platform, and although John was meant be in first class, he became so engrossed in our conversation that he ended up coming and sitting with me and the plebs. It was wonderful – we talked and talked the whole way down. I told him about my master's degree and all the ideas I had about FM, then he asked me what I was planning to do when I finished the course. I told him that I didn't really know, I just wanted to make a difference to the industry.

"Have you ever thought about coming into a private company and doing it from the other side?" he asked me.

I told him that I hadn't – to be honest, those of us on the 'client' side tended to think that outsourcing people wore horns back then. You didn't really trust them, because they were always trying to sell you stuff.

"Well," he said, "if you ever do start thinking about it, please get in touch with me, because we'd be very interested in you joining us."

I told him I would think about it, but in the meantime, there was something he could help me with. I was doing my dissertation on the human resources side of FM, because for me it was all about the people, and I really wanted to do a case study about the outsourcing sector.

"Would you be willing to nominate somebody in your company to help me out?" I asked him.

"Of course I will," he said. And that was that. He put me in touch with a wonderful woman called Margaret Drury, who was Procord's HR director, and Ian Mills and Dave Burnett, who were on the operations side, and they helped me research and write a really good dissertation.

When I passed my MSc in 1994, it was one of the proudest moments of my life. Doing that master's was amazing for me, because it gave me the confidence that I knew what I was talking about. It also allowed my brain to expand into strategic thinking. Beforehand, I had been very practical and operational, but now I was able to look at the bigger picture. I could see more clearly where clients were coming from and how everything fitted together.

Because I now had this enlarged perspective, I decided that it was the right time for me to move on from the RPMS. Almost immediately, I found myself being headhunted by five different outsourcing companies, one of which was Procord. After doing some research, I narrowed it down to two – Procord and a cleaning company. I went to see the managing director of the cleaning company, which offered me a very good deal as an operations director. I told them I would think about it, then I went to spend a day at Procord.

Of course, I knew them pretty well by then, and at the end of the day, I sat down with Margaret Drury, the HR lady. She came straight to the point.

"Well, if you want to join us, we need to talk money, don't we?" she said.

"Yes," I replied, "I suppose we do. I have been considering another company and I know what they offered me, so I have an idea of what my market value might be, but if the deal is right, I would like to join you guys."

"The deal will be right," she said, "because we want you, so what do you want?" I said I'd prefer it if she said what she thought I was worth before I revealed what the other company had offered me. She then offered me £10,000 more than that, plus a car, which I'd never had in any previous job.

"At that level, I'd be very interested," I said, and that was that. Within a week, we had signed the documentation and I had given my three months' notice in to the RPMS.

I was really proud of what I'd achieved there. I'd been in that job for six years, and I know for one of them I'd been ill, but I'd transformed the way FM worked in the school and had several articles written about me in the press. Neil Gershon wrote me a lovely letter saying that they were very sorry to see me go but absolutely delighted for me. Then he asked me what I wanted as a leaving present. I had just bought a house – we'll come back to that in a moment – and I told him that what I'd really like was cash, so I could spend it on that. I was expecting something like £50, but they raised £400 for me and gave it to me at my leaving do. I was very touched. It was a fantastic evening. A lot of the top professors came, including Robert Winston, the famous IVF pioneer. He was great fun – he used to run the hospital pantomime – and we had become pals.

It would be too simplistic to say that from here on in my life was a case of 'happy ever after,' but this is definitely when things really started to come together. I'd got my master's, I'd been headhunted and was just about to start a new job with a salary double what I'd had before, plus a car. I'd also finally got back on the property ladder, after a long break.

I'd had to sell the Hackney flat to buy Sam out. I don't begrudge that now at all, because he has been a rock for my daughters, and he and his partner are lovely people, but I was deeply pissed off about it at the time. Then I'd bought a nightmare place in Walthamstow, which kept getting burgled. One night, the man who ran the local folk club drove me back there, and when I put the key in the lock, I couldn't open it because someone on the other side had put the safety chain on. The folk club guy then guy did a flying karate kick, burst the door open, and saw a burglar running out of the French doors. Eventually, I'd sold the place to Elayna (it had got safer by then), but this had put me in serious negative equity, so for several years I'd been renting in Greenford, near my friend Fiona.

Then, right at the end of my time at the RPMS, a house just around the corner came on the market for £65,000. I was almost able to afford it, because they were doing negative equity mortgages in those days, but even after raising loans up to the max, I was still short by about £2,000. Then one day, this guy at the RPMS who was very attracted to me, just said, "I can give you that money."

"Don't be so stupid," I told him, "you can't possibly give me that money. That's just totally unethical."

He said, "To be honest, I've got my own business that is earning quite a lot of money and if I pay you as a consultant it will all be tax deductible and it won't cost me a penny."

If it wasn't going to cost him anything, I thought "OK" and said yes. I couldn't believe anyone could be that generous.

So, talk about pivotal moments. Have I used my wiles as a woman at times? Yes. Am I proud of it? YES! I did what I had to do. I had a hunger within me to survive and to make a better life for myself and my girls, because they were both still struggling. I just wanted things to be better.

Anyway, I moved into the house in Stanley Avenue in Greenford, and my father paid to put a new kitchen in for me. I re-did the garden and Steve from the RPMS came and did a lot of work for me. I was very, very happy there. And shortly after moving in, I met Vin, the man who would end up becoming my third husband.

We met at the Station Tavern in Latimer Road, at Bob's Blues Club, which was a very famous London venue. I never sang or played there, but they had a house band who were absolutely brilliant. Every Sunday lunchtime, I used to go down there with a whole crowd of friends and have a jolly good time. Vin lived locally, so he was always in there, and that's how we met. We just used to smile and say hello. Then this young couple – an Italian girl and her English boyfriend, who had befriended me in the pub and knew that I sang – decided that they wanted a scratch band for their wedding. So, they asked me if I would do the singing and Vin if he would do the playing, along with the drummer and the bass player from the pub house band. Then all four of us went to Italy to play at this wedding.

The two guys in the scratch band said that they could jam along to anything and that Vin and I should choose the songs and they would just come in behind us. So, I went round to Vin's flat and fell in love with him immediately. Or perhaps it was lust at first, because he was drop-dead gorgeous and still is!

I really wanted to meet somebody, although officially by the time I met Vin I had finished with men. I'd tried dating through an introductions agency and met this guy who was a widower. He and his wife had been in the Zeebrugge ferry disaster – he'd been holding her hand when she'd slipped away and died. I was damaged goods myself after the breakdown and all the rest of it, so we were absolutely horrendous together. He did drive me all the way up to Colchester to see my father before he died though. My stepmother and I sat on each side of him while he slipped away. That was in 1994, before I got the Procord job with the car.

After that, I said to myself, "That's it, I'm not doing this introduction agency thing anymore, because it's dangerous. You don't know who you are dealing with and I'm just too trusting." As far as I was concerned, I'd finished with men. But Vin changed my mind about that. Still, it was an on-and-off relationship for some time and we didn't get married until 2002. By this time, we had moved into a house in Ravenor Park Road that was ours rather than just mine and was the perfect venue for our reception.

One week after my leaving do at the RPMS, I was working for Procord as a senior account manager for British Gas. I was looking after 14 buildings in London, including the huge headquarters near Marble Arch, and two in Solihull. Or rather, I was working for Johnson Controls (JCL), a huge multinational FM company that had just bought Procord in a deal that had made John Jack and the other top people there millionaires.

It was just at the time when British Gas was being privatised. There was a huge redundancy programme, because they were very top heavy with management, and the privatisation meant that they needed to cut their costs. They were also going to get rid of their properties in London and move their headquarters to Slough. I managed the decommissioning of buildings, as well as keeping them going as long as the head office staff were still in them.

It was fantastic. I had a building manager in each one of the properties who reported into me, plus a catering contracts manager, a maintenance manager and a cleaning contracts manager. I had been used to running the whole thing myself and thought, "This is easy-peasy." But I did learn to be more strategic and financially adept.

My success in this role resulted in JCL asking me to go to troubleshoot a contract that was in trouble in the marketing sector. I sorted this out successfully and then was selected as a candidate to run the prestigious JCL BP contract at Sunbury. They liked my presentation and I won the job!

Within a few weeks of my joining, I went off to do a 10-day study trip in the USA to see how they did FM over there. There were five of us. We went to JCL head office, so we met the guy who ran the whole global operation, and everywhere we went we were wined and dined by very important people in the company. I had only been in the BP role for a short time and I felt really intimidated, because I was the only woman. I was still fairly fragile behind my confident facade, and I found it very challenging, but it was great.

We went to an insurance company office in Michigan, where the guy in charge ran it like *The Stepford Wives* – he was a bloke and all the admin people were women. When they came in, they had to take their shoes off and put plastic bags on their feet so they wouldn't make the carpets dirty. It was just mind-blowing.

Then we went down to NASA in Florida, where we saw a rocket being launched. We also went to San Francisco and visited Microsoft and Sun Microsystems. Everywhere we went, we were taking notes about what we thought we might be able to bring over to the UK from the US. But actually, it turned out we were way ahead of them. It was strange, because FM had come out of the US, but the concepts were far more developed in the UK. The States had elected to keep the division between technical and soft services, whereas in the UK, the likes of Procord had bundled them together, creating synergies and multi-tasking the front-line staff, which saved money and increased efficiency.

Just after I had the breakdown, but before I went back to work, I'd done a counselling course. At that time, I didn't know if I was going to keep my job, so I was determined to prepare myself for a different career in case I needed one. But I just wasn't ready for it – it was all too raw, and I kept collapsing in tears all the time, so I had to give it up. Nevertheless, the time I spent on the course stood me in great stead for managing big teams. At the RPMS I'd had maybe 40 people directly reporting to me but at British Gas, I had well over 100. By the time I got to BP, the figure was probably nearer to 300. Having that kind of counselling background was incredibly helpful when it came to understanding people and how to talk to them, particularly when they were in trouble or struggling.

I was very defensive of the people who worked for me. Like a good football manager, I would back up my staff in public, then beat them up when I got them in a room on their own and make them apologise and put things right. But I came to realise that very few people get out of bed in the morning intending to have a crap day and do everything wrong. If you inspire them to do the best that they can and give them the right tools and instructions, they go away at the end of the day happy, and ultimately that has an effect on society as a whole.

There was a young chap at JCL who had started off as a carpenter, but he was really good at IT, so they had made him into an IT consultant. Anyway, he was quite newly married, and I called him into my office one day, because he hadn't done something for me that I had asked him to do, and I needed it for a meeting later that day. I would never sit somebody across the desk from me, because it would put a physical barrier between us, so I brought my chair around and sat next to him.

Then I said, "I'm really disappointed. You said that you would be able to get such and such to me by today but you haven't. Why? Tell me why."

He then burst into tears. He had been overworked by JCL and was being pulled and pushed from pillar to post doing consultancy work when he was actually supposed to be working on my contract. Because he was ambitious, he wanted to do what was right for the company and he wasn't doing what he was actually being paid to do as part of his employment. So, I decided not to bollock him. Instead, I counselled him for around an hour. I told him that he had to learn to stand up to people, or else he would burn himself out within a year and be no use to anybody. He took it on board and today he is a very senior IT guy in one of the leading FM companies. I am really proud of him.

It was a dream job. BP Sunbury was a huge site, with about 80 buildings covering all three main parts of the company – oil, chemicals and explorations – and I managed the whole thing, leading not only my own subcontractors, but all the outsourced contractors on site. The site manager, Martin Wells, was absolutely brilliant and a great guy.

After a while, Esso came to BP to do a peer review – in the oil industry, they did that a lot, because they learned from each other that way. In particular, they wanted to see how we were doing property and FM at BP, because they had an outsourced contract with JCL which they weren't very happy with. BP told Esso that they were delighted with the way I was managing their site. We all got on famously and I took them round and showed them everything. Then they said to JCL, "We want Anne to do what she's done at BP for us."

I went to Esso and the client thought I did a great job for them for over a year. I had a big staff, and it was very different from BP. That had been one site, but now I had the whole Esso portfolio to look after – distribution centres, all the office and admin, everything except the oil refineries. I was travelling all over the place. I also helped to set up the very first pay-as-you-go petrol station in the UK for them. I had a great client and a great team and enjoyed my time there immensely.

Then the new guys who were managing JCL asked me to lead their bid for a contract with Cisco, the IT networking firm. The way that they persuaded me to do it was by saying that if we won the bid, I would get the job of operations director. So, I went along with it and did really well – we won the bid. Then they told me not only that I wasn't going to get the job they had promised me, but I wasn't going back to Esso either. Instead, they were moving me to an insurance company called AON. I was devastated. I'd done all these wonders at BP and Esso, but felt they just kept kicking me in the teeth. And the false promise of promotion was like McDonald's all over again.

I must have been very close to another breakdown at that point. I started seeing Dr Zigmond again, and this time I took Vin with me, because he was struggling with his drinking. My physical health wasn't good either. In 1999, I'd gone down with polymyalgia, which meant that I could hardly walk. I went off to AON and was eventually given the job of operations director, but by this time, my relationship with JCL was fatally damaged. Around Christmas 2001, I was off sick again – this time I had throat thrush, which was horrible – and in early 2002, JCL and I agreed to part company.

Vin and I were both in a much better place after seeing David Zigmond for a while, and after we'd won the Cisco bid, he proposed to me. It happened at the very plush Stafford Hotel, just next to the Ritz, where JCL had put up everyone involved in the Cisco bid after giving us a big dinner and taking us to *Miss Saigon* to thank us. I hadn't been expecting the proposal at all. I had always assumed that, because Vin was 13 years younger than me, sooner or later, knowing my luck, we would just split up. So when he got down on one knee and asked me to marry him, it was a real 'oh my God' moment. I just couldn't say no to him.

We were busily planning our wedding when the JCL relationship issues came to a head. At this point, we had to make some big decisions very quickly. Were we still going ahead with the wedding and where were we going to live? We knew there wouldn't be any more money coming in for a while as I had decided to take a year-long sabbatical. Fortunately, we'd bought a little cottage in Dawley in Telford in Shropshire in February, the month before this all happened. I loved the area – when I'd been singing with Sam, we'd toured around there a lot – and we had some great friends called David and Maggie Hunt (aka 'Doctor Sunshine'), who we stayed with while we looked at properties. In the end, we bought this fabulous little two-bedroom place for about £37,000. It was riddled with damp but it had great potential. It was supposed to be our retirement home, and a holiday place for us in the meantime, but we decided that we could always move there permanently if we had to.

Anyway, we went ahead and had the most wonderful wedding, at Osterley Park. We had decided: "Look, we're only going to get married once, let's just do it, let's just have the day of our lives." It was absolutely magical! We had champagne on the west lawn, a reception in our garden and then we went on honeymoon to Cyprus taking our bear, Ted Neads with us. Ted had been a Christmas present in 1999 and had become our mediator and peacekeeper. I won't go into all that now, but Ted is a real character with his own wardrobe and Facebook page. Known locally as the foul-mouthed bear, he has travelled all over the world with us.

When we got back, we decided to move into the cottage in Telford and see what happened. We'd been able to buy it outright, so even if I couldn't find any more work, at least we'd have a roof over our heads. We couldn't move in right away though, so for the time being we'd carry on living in the house in Ravenor Park Road in Greenford. We'd put it on the market, and commute to Shropshire to do up the cottage.

Dave Burnett and Ian Mills of Procord. Both helped me with my MSc dissertation

One of my proudest moments – gaining my MSc in Facilities and Environmental Management, 1994

Neil Gershon and me at my RPMS leaving do, 1995

Early days in my relationship with Vin, 1996

With my friend and colleague Marilyn Standley, a very special person who taught me so much

12

IT AIN'T WHAT YOU DO,
IT'S THE WAY THAT YOU DO IT

Yes, I'm a self-made woman and I know my own mind
Be a self-made woman and get to know your own mind
It won't make you easy, but it might make you kind!
— Anne Lennox-Martin, *Self-Made Woman*

I t was strange for me not working, because I had never been in a situation before where I'd had time off without being ill, but I remember the period after our wedding as a magical time. Vin had got a job teaching toddlers IT skills, and he was brilliant at it. The parents and the children adored him, and he was as happy as the day was long. It was part-time though, which allowed us to go up to Telford on Thursday and then come back in time for him to go to work on Monday.

Once we'd sold the house in Greenford, we moved into the cottage in Dawley full-time. Then we found and purchased this wonderful, dilapidated, slightly larger place in Telford, which we called Higgledy-Piggledy Cottage. The plan was for us to do it up, then move into it and either sell or rent out the Dawley place. Much of my 'sabbatical' was spent helping Vin to renovate H-P Cottage, which we eventually moved into in July 2003.

By then, I had just about begun my very first job as a solo consultant, for Kingston University. Once I'd moved up to Shropshire, I'd realised that there weren't actually any FM jobs in the area, not even in Birmingham, so I'd decided that I would offer to do some training. JCL had used me for internal training – I'd run the graduate programme for them, which I absolutely loved – and I'd also put everybody at BP through a customer care programme, which they had then got me to do for other accounts. So I was already an experienced trainer, and doing more of it made sense.

This first training was about implementing service level agreements. I'd already started talking to my friend Marilyn Standley about us doing something together, but she hadn't actually won any business yet for her Facio Consult business. Our first joint venture was a project at Sheffield University. Then we got a really good contract with Sky Television. Marilyn went in as the interim head of property and estates, I came in as change manager and another friend of ours called Linda came in as the operational manager. We were a triumvirate of women and we sorted most things out.

When I got to Sky's headquarters in Isleworth, the first thing I did was what I always do when I get a new FM contract: familiarise myself with what my clients are doing and work out how they could do it better. How can we engage the people working there and make them realise how important they are? One of my mantras was "It ain't what you do, it's the way that you do it," and that's what I try to convey to my clients. So, I went in and did a gap analysis of how we could make the services more streamlined to please the customers.

Sky was great, because there were so many problems that were incredibly easy to solve. For example, it was a 24/7 operation, but the mail room was only open from 8 a.m. to 4 p.m. A lot of the recordings they used, particularly for the sports channels, came in from outside broadcasts. So the tapes or discs or whatever would be delivered out of hours and either there'd be no one to sign for them or they'd get left on the windowsill at the mail room, with nobody knowing that they were there. It wasn't at all difficult to fix. We just told the courier firms that when they came in out of hours, they were to leave the packages at the gatehouse. Security would sign for them, then they would ring sports, who would send somebody to the gatehouse to get them. It was so simple and there was no cost, so they were over the moon.

Sky also had a lot of people who worked part-time in

the evenings, but the catering service closed at 4 p.m., so they couldn't get anything to eat. We stretched the way the catering worked, and got skeleton crews in to provide things like soup and jacket potatoes out of hours. That was really well received. We also bought a job lot of those pub-style table/benches from B&Q and put them all around the site. This enabled the staff to have meetings in the fresh air, which they loved.

Another problem that it didn't take Einstein to resolve was correcting a ridiculous situation in which the helpdesk was only open from 9 a.m. to 5 p.m. in an organisation that ran 24/7. Sky were growing so rapidly that all focus was being put into operations and sales, and they hadn't realised how dependent their core business was on facilities. It was wonderfully satisfying to be able to make such a difference. When I left, the client manager presented me with three roses. I've still got them today – I've dug them up from every garden I've had and transplanted them.

Our most important contract was with the Met Police. It was also probably the most enjoyable of the lot – I loved that job! Marilyn was well known to Ernst & Young, who had been asked by the Met to find some operational FM consultants to augment the team working on the second generation of outsourcing they were planning. Luckily, she nominated me! As a team, we ran various workshops with the Met property team and then our core team worked out the future property and FM strategy of the police in London more or less on the back of a fag packet (actually, it was more like a flip chart, as I remember).

The Met were very keen on resilience and frightened of having one contractor doing everything. They just didn't want to run that risk. So we developed a model for them, which has survived to this day, of having one outsourced contract for the south of London, another one in the north and a third one which would run the helpdesk and provide one version of the truth in terms of data. It would also operate as the coordinator for the other two outsourced providers. The work we were doing covered all the police stations, the dog-handling units, the stables, custody suites, you name it. Six hundred different buildings. And it was fantastic, because there was so much that we could do to improve things. This third contract has developed over the years to become 'the Integrator Model'.

The area that I was particularly responsible for transforming was the cleaning. The Met property department was mostly staffed by men and a lot of them were ex-police officers who had no interest in cleaning at all. Like many public sector organisations at the time, they had 20 of them doing one thing where one would do. At the same time, other areas would be totally neglected as they were not perceived as important.

I don't know if I dare say this, but frankly, the cleaning in the Met was a disgrace. I went to visit police stations where your shoes would stick to the floor because of the filth.

You would go into cells that would be covered in faeces, because the prisoners would throw it at security cameras, or just smear the walls with it. The head offices received a reasonable but not very good level of cleaning, but the police stations were appalling. There were around 12 different companies running the cleaning across London, with about 20 contracts, all with different specifications. And nobody had been managing it, because they all wanted to see themselves as property guys and thought cleaning was beneath them – whereas I was steeped in it all and I loved it. I had made it at Hammersmith Hospital on the cleaning side, so I thought, "I can get stuck into this – this is going to be no problem whatsoever."

The biggest issue was the cells. A lot of the occupants were messy, to put it mildly. Many of them were drug or alcohol addicts, who were constantly throwing up everywhere, and if you raised one of the mattresses in the cells, you would find any number of pubic hairs stuck to the underside. Then there was the blanket problem. The distribution system was all over the place, and often the blanket given to a new arrival in a cell would still be warm from the previous occupant.

The Met had lay visitors coming in to make sure the prisoners were being treated decently and that their human rights were being addressed. What they'd often find was vulnerable people without blankets in cells covered in sick. Naturally, they were giving the chief constables and the assistant commissioner a lot of grief about this – and threatening to publicise it. Meanwhile, the Met had just become the responsibility of the mayor, so there was a lot of politics around the issue.

The root of the problem was that the pressure on the police stations in London was enormous, particularly in the old-fashioned Victorian places. There were so many people being put into custody that they could rarely release the cells to let the cleaners in. When they were empty, there would often be no cleaners on duty. And even when they could get in, they weren't always very good at the job. They were all on minimum wage and you'd get these people in their seventies toddling around with buckets and mops.

Something urgently needed to be done. The first thing I did was get all the contracted cleaning companies in a room together, which was unheard of. "Look," I told them, "these are the issues, this is how we are going to work it out together, and you either come on board with me or you're out." Then we had to change the way that the police stations worked. We had to build bridges with the custody sergeants and develop systems for making sure that the cleaners had regular access to the cells. I also revolutionised the distribution of blankets. We retendered the contract, got a new company in, and explained to them what the problem was. Then we introduced a 'just in time' delivery system, so that there would almost always be enough stock available. If there wasn't, which could happen – sometimes they'd have six people passing through a cell in one day – they could pay to get an emergency supply of blankets delivered within four hours, whereas before they'd had to wait a week for their next routine order.

So the Met job was absolutely brilliant. Afterwards, Alan Croney, the former director of property and FM at the Met, wrote a lovely tribute to what I'd achieved there:

Anne communicates in a totally convincing and game changing way to break established moulds and build on people skills at all levels. She has an amazing ability to release potential across the FM spectrum. It has been a great privilege to work with Anne over many years and without her impact my own achievements would have been seriously lower. The FM industry needs the rare skills Anne possesses.

In 2005, Marilyn and I helped our colleague Lucy Jeynes to set up Women In FM, a mentoring, networking, support and events group which was part of the British Institute of Facilities Management (BIFM). I was doing a lot of training and consultancy for the British Institute for FM, through its joint venture with an FM training firm called Quadrilect. I'd been one of the founder members of the BIFM back in 1993 and Marilyn had been the first chair. Back then, I had always showed up to the AGM to make sure there was a quorum, because it was difficult to get people to attend at first, but today the BIFM has morphed into the Institute of Workplace and FM and has over 17,000 members. Over the years, I've had lots of fascinating training work through them, ranging from The National Grid to the Scottish Parliament, most of it majored on customer service and change management.

My next major assignment was working with Martin Pickard, who wrote that poem at the start of chapter 10. I'd known him since my early days on the conference circuit back in the early 90s – we'd always been the last two out of the bar! He'd gone on to start a business called FM Guru, which did lots of consultancy work. He and a very dear friend called Sarah Hodge asked me to come in and help set up a company called NB Entrust to do the FM for Nelson Bakewell, a very large residential property investment company who were managing agents for several big pension companies. They wanted to revolutionise the way they provided integrated property and FM, so they got Martin in as the consultant to work out how to do that. They formed this new company, and I did a lot of the training and created the front-line service ambassador role. It was fabulous!

During this time, Vin and I were working on our relationship and enjoying some great travels abroad. We visited many places in Europe as well as Egypt, China and Thailand, and more were to follow. For someone who only flew on their first aeroplane at the age of 38, it was sheer heaven. But Vin's drinking was getting worse and in 2007, he took the brave step of going into rehab. He has never drunk a single drop of alcohol since.

In 2008, we did a Neuro-Linguistic Programming

(NLP) course together. I thought it would be good for our relationship and it was. It would take another book to describe exactly what NLP is, but I wrote an article about it called 'NLP – A Great Tool for Professional FM's', and the first paragraph should give you some idea what it's all about:

NLP has often been called an instruction manual for the unconscious. It is a body of knowledge (some unique, some pulled from other respected sources) which combines with a series of tools to enable any of us to improve the way we think; the strategies we use to achieve our goals and our relationships with other people.

I am now a qualified NLP Master Practitioner and have found it incredibly useful in my work in FM.

Since the mid-noughties, I've never really looked back. In 2007, the magazine *FM World* selected me as one of the 20 most influential women in the industry. Then in 2013 came the high point of my whole career, when I was given the 'Profound Impact on the FM Industry Over the Last Five Years Award' by the BIFM (I mentioned before how I made sure Neil Gershon and David Zigmond were on my table for the ceremony). The following year, I was awarded an Eminence Fellowship of the Royal Institution of Chartered Surveyors. At that time, only three people had ever been Fellows of both BIFM and RICS, and just one of them had been a woman – me!

In 2014, I founded a new company called FMP360. It

was what I described as a 'collaborative consultancy'. The basic idea was that clients always measure their suppliers, but I believe it should also work the other way round. That way, both sides gain insight into how they are doing and how they are perceived. I got a good friend called David Emanuel to develop a software system for me which sent out surveys every quarter for both clients and suppliers to fill in. Then the consultant (i.e. me) would write a report identifying the hotspots, what needed addressing, what was going awry and what was going well. We had some really good clients, like Channel 4, the Ministry of Justice (although they turned out not to be relationship-orientated so it couldn't possibly work), and a very forward-thinking pharmaceutical company. But the company itself never really took off. I had a wonderful board of directors – absolutely top people in FM like David, Seamus Grealish and Lucy Jeynes – but we had no salespeople, and that was the heart of the problem.

I wouldn't say it was a failure though. Before I set up FMP360, collaboration wasn't much talked about in the industry. Now it's all the rage. One of the consultants who worked with me said, "You should never think that what you did between 2014 and 2018 was not something that actually made a difference, because it really did. Now everybody talks about relationships and collaboration and you were a pioneer in that field." But we couldn't make it pay. There just wasn't enough money to sustain the model that we tried to put in place.

Subsequently, I've probably been best known for doing change management consultancy through my own company, Anne Lennox-Martin Ltd. Essentially, I'll take a rather tired FM operation and turn it into something a bit more sexy and exciting. I've done that more in the higher education sector than anywhere else. Working with one of the best clients I have ever had, Mike Sheppard, I ran 'The Journey Towards Service Excellence' in two major universities, with measurable success. When it finished around Christmas 2020, this felt like the best time to wrap up my companies and start a new phase in my life.

Third time lucky! Vin and I marry in 2002

Receiving my BIFM Award in 2013

Receiving my RICS Eminence Fellowship in 2014

Receiving the Freedom of the City of London 2018

EPILOGUE
A SHROPSHIRE LASS

I have now entered into Transition! You can't call it retirement as the one thing I do know is that I couldn't sit around doing nothing. Just being a little old lady doing her garden wouldn't suit me, although I love gardening and do a lot of it. I've recently started a course with In Touch and the Institute of Leadership and Management on coaching for executives. I may use it for earning, which would be nice, or I might use it for voluntary stuff, but I'll definitely do something with it. Even in terms of self-development and growth, it's a good thing to have under my belt.

I had to give up singing about three years ago, but I did form a band when we first moved up here, with Vin, Bill Caddick and a couple of others. Surprise, surprise, it was called The Anne Lennox-Martin Band! We did gigs and made an album, but eventually I had to give it up because of throat problems. At one point in the past, I had lost my voice completely for three months. People kept saying to Vin, "Haha! That must be fun, she can't speak!" and he'd get really upset with them, because it was absolutely awful. The only way we could communicate was by writing things down on paper.

Although music has fallen by the wayside, I've got plenty to keep me busy. Everything's fun to me. I'm never bored and don't understand people who are.

There's never enough time to do everything that I want to do. I love spending time with Vin, and we've got our little property empire to look after (we've got eight houses now that we rent out). And I'm absolutely besotted with my grandchildren. Elayna has four children and Mickie has one, and they all get a special day with 'Missy' (as they call me) once a year. We also have Matt, who Vin brought up while he was in a previous relationship. He has adopted us as his official parents and we call him our 'Chosen Son'. Matt and his family live in the North East and we have plenty of FaceTime capers with them.

This book is really a homage to a life that has turned out so well, despite all the hardships along the way. It's a celebration of survival and of finding happiness. Vin is my absolute soulmate, and our life together is full of laughter and love. Even in the current Covid-19 pandemic we have found a peace and tranquillity in our walks together and just being us.

So many people in FM have told me that the tale of my career and how I got into it has been an inspiration for them. When I've told them about my past, a lot of the young women I've mentored have said, "Oh my God, what a story! You must write a book." Well, now I have. It's been difficult to choose what to keep out and what to leave in, but I've done my best to cover the major ups and downs.

People sometimes ask me if I got anything from all the awards I received in the latter part of my career. My answer is "a sense of wonder". When I think back on the past – the Scientology years, being homeless in Regent's Park, working as a cleaner for all those years – climbing to the top of my industry and being able to put letters after my name seems almost funny. It's a miracle. It's a kind of magic.

Even though a lot of my life has been very traumatic, I wouldn't change it at all. Every step I have taken, forward, backward and sideways, has led me to where I am today. And I like myself. Me and I get on really well together, and you can't really ask for more than that.

Singing in Shropshire, 2006

With my husband and soulmate, Vin, on an outing in London during the Pandemic, 2020

StoryTerrace

CPSIA information can be obtained
at www.ICGtesting.com
Printed in the USA
BVHW021404041021
618090BV00023B/927